A Short History of
TASMANIA

A Short History of
TASMANIA

Lloyd Robson

MELBOURNE
OXFORD UNIVERSITY PRESS
OXFORD   AUCKLAND   NEW YORK

OXFORD UNIVERSITY PRESS
Oxford New York Toronto
Delhi Bombay Calcutta Madras Karachi
Kuala Lumpur Singapore Hong Kong Tokyo
Nairobi Dar es Salaam Cape Town
Melbourne Auckland
and associates in
Beirut Berlin Ibadan Mexico City Nicosia

National Library of Australia
Cataloguing-in-Publication data:

Robson, L. L. (Leslie Lloyd), 1931–
A short history of Tasmania.

Includes index.
ISBN 0 19 554651 2.

1. Tasmania – History.   I. Title.

994.6

Edited by Janet McKenzie
Typeset in Kuala Lumpur by Syarikat Seng Teik Sdn. Bhd.
Printed in Singapore
Published by Oxford University Press, 7 Bowen Crescent, Melbourne
OXFORD is a trademark of Oxford University Press

Contents

Note: As this is an historical work, imperial measures have been retained throughout.

List of Illustrations

of the Launceston merchants, Johnstone & Wilmot. Tasmanian Collection.

Page 97 W. L. Neale (1853–1913), Tasmanian Director of Education 1904–09. *Tasmanian Mail*, 14 January 1905, p. 22. National Library of Australia.

Page 102 Joseph Aloysius Lyons (1879–1939). Photograph, n.d. National Library of Australia.

Page 105 Dame Enid Lyons (née Burnell) (1897–1981). Wedding day, 28 April 1915. National Library of Australia.

Page 109 Beattie, J. W. & Co. *Hobart. Souvenir of the 40th Battalion* (Launceston, 'Examiner' and 'Weekly Courier', 1916). Photograph on page 3: The Battalion on Parade. Tasmanian Collection.

Page 111 Conscription Plebiscite 1917. Poster. National Library of Australia.

Page 113 Father O'Donnell (1877–1949), Alex Gurney, *Tasmanians today* (Hobart, Mercury, 1926). Tasmanian Collection.

Page 121 A. G. Ogilvie (1892–1939). Alex Gurney, *Tasmanians today* (Hobart, Mercury, 1926). Tasmanian Collection.

Page 128 Lyndhurst Falkiner Giblin (1872–1951). Photograph, n.d. National Library of Australia.

Page 131 Multiple Arch Dam, Miena, Great Lake. Spurlings Pty Ltd. *Launceston. Tasmania illustrated: a complete pictorial record containing 122 views of all parts of the garden island.* (Launceston, 'Examiner' and 'Weekly Courier' Offices, c. 1927)

Page 134 South Burnie and the Paper Mills, fronting Emu Bay. *The Advocate Annual: Tasmania illustrated* (Burnie, The Advocate, 1939), p. 24.

Page 137 Sir Ivan Holyman (1896–1957), co-founder of Australian National Airways Pty Ltd. Photograph, n.d. National Library of Australia.

Page 139 Sir Herbert William Gepp (1877–1954), general manager of Electrolytic Zinc Co. 1917–23. Photograph. Electrolytic Zinc Company of Australasia Ltd.

Page 140 Cadbury's Chocolate Factory, Claremont, 1921. Photograph. Cadbury Schweppes Pty Ltd.

Page 146 Tasmanian Bismark Potatoes. 'Blue Eyes' brand. Potato Marketing Board advertising card, n.d. Tasmanian Collection.

Page 150 Wrest Point Riviera Hotel, Hobart, 1945. *The Examiner Annual: 1945* (Launceston, The Examiner, 1945). Tasmanian Collection.

Preface

Any short history by its nature demands a certain boldness in presentation and selection of material and themes; stern experts will doubtless bring careful study to bear on areas judged to demand more attention, in their judgement. The nature of the writing of history in and about Australia has changed and is changing very rapidly in comparison with the work produced in the period to around the early 1960s, and it is in the nature of analysis of the past for fashions to come and go and fresh insights be offered.

All written histories reflect the experience and assumptions of the writer, and to that extent any historical work will reveal to the perceptive reader a good deal about the times in which the history was written, and possibly disclose more about the writer than he might expect. The author is willy-nilly a standing target but this is as it should be if our understanding of the past is to enrich and broaden our knowledge of the present. There are no holy custodians of the past, gifted with the ability to call the shots in the present and future. The world around us has always been dissolving and differences of opinion about what is significant should lead to further constructive work in the field.

The overall theme of this Short History is the establishment in Van Diemen's Land/Tasmania of part of that restless society which has emerged from Europe since the seventeenth century and spread itself across the globe, suffused with the ideology of Christianity and increasingly equipped with powerful technology.

The pattern is largely that of colonialism, conceived in terms of the exploitation which the word evokes, and the essential duality of the colony/state in its relationship to the colonizing authority. The implications of the term 'colonist' are everywhere in the history of the British Empire and Sir Keith Hancock's felicitous term 'transplanted Britons' is nowhere more evident in Australia than in the case of the island state.

Tasmania developed as a stereotype colony and the interlocking of British and colonial interests dominate its history. The economy of the colony and state for nearly all its past since European settlement was steered by the needs of the metropolitan authority established in London. In political terms, Tasmania sought to emulate British parliamentary practice and procedure, except that whereas the second House of Parliament in Britain had its wings clipped in the Edwardian period, the Legislative Council of Tasmania continued to set the parameters of political action to such an extent that its conduct came to be judged as not remarkable.

All this was aided greatly by Tasmanians' perception of their weak and isolated position out on the very edge of the Empire. This was the principal factor which sharpened loyalty to Britain, so that the great European civil wars which commenced in 1914 and in 1939 inevitably drew Australia (and hence Tasmania), as an economic and cultural dependency, into those conflicts in the same way as other dependencies and trading partners were involved.

Yet there developed in the island some indications of a local character and style, not a little associated with the important fact that the colony/state was an island, the inhabitants of which were always, like all islanders, suspicious of outsiders and a little envious of the wider world and its preoccupations and developments. At the same time, the rugged landscape of Tasmania led to regional identity and interests.

The violent and bloody origins of European settlement in Tasmania have only recently come to be explored in terms of how Tasmanians see themselves, and it is to be hoped that this Short History may go some way further towards an understanding of the past and, therefore, of the present and future, both for Europeans and for Aborigines. If we perceive the past refracted through a distorted lens, we falsify our present perceptions and react to false resonances of the past.

I wish particularly to thank my publishers for their initiative and tactful silences, especially Louise Sweetland and Sarah Dawson. Janet Mckenzie employed editorial skills of a high quality and the Department of History at the University of Melbourne helped greatly with financial assistance. Geoffrey Stilwell at the Allport Library and Museum of Fine Arts in Hobart was, as ever, an invaluable source of information, as were Barbara Valentine and Margaret Glover. Geoff Scrivener at the Morris Miller Library, University of Tasmania, greatly assisted me by so readily making available material embodied in theses, full details of which will appear in Volume 2 of my *History of Tasmania*. Dick Marriott drew the maps and I also wish to thank the Electrolytic Zinc Company and Cadbury Schweppes for locating illustrations. Professor A. G. L. Shaw used his good offices in securing permission to reproduce the portrait of Governor Arthur.

1

Invasion

During the last 100 000 years or so, the sun has grown hotter and then cooler, so that the sea rose and fell, and the land masses of the planet have changed shape and position. Sometimes the area of Tasmania has been a peninsula of Australia Proper, sometimes an island. Humans probably were in the area some 40 000 years ago and certainly 20 000 years ago were on the Bassian Plain, land now beneath the seas of east and central Bass Strait. Indeed, they were further south, and subsisted in what is now central Tasmania, on the very edge of the glacial regions; perhaps this is the furthest south ever reached by early peoples.

About 12 000 years ago the seas rose again, cutting off such people as lived in the peninsula/island of Tasmania. It may be that these groups had lived in the area for much longer than 12 000 years but their relationship with other Australian peoples is not known. They did not possess the dingo, however, which suggests that the Tasmanian peoples certainly were isolated before that animal became prevalent in the north . . . but none of this is known for certain. The culture and development of the people of the island can only be reconstructed from some most preliminary archaeological work and from the fleeting moment in time when the Aborigines came under notice of their European conquerors.

Between 4000 and 6000 persons appear to have supported themselves on the island at the time of European arrival, but the figure is speculative. In the 1830s, G. A. Robinson in the course of his travels recorded every Aboriginal he could find and discovered that he could enumerate no more than about 300. This suggests an even more substantial death-rate if estimates of original numbers of Aborigines seriously fail to take into account the impact of introduced diseases.

The island on which the Aborigines were stranded some 12 000 years ago was 26 000 square miles and situated between 40 and 43.5 degrees south latitude. It was a land of innumerable streams, rivers and mountains with a heavy rainfall on the western side, shading off to the east, brought by the prevailing westerlies which blew, unimpeded, halfway across the southern oceans. The next land to the westward was in the region of Cape Horn. As the mighty glaciers melted and moved, they left enormous numbers of tiny lakes in the central west areas of the mountainous hinterland. From this area of extremely high rainfall derived very powerful rivers, the principal one to become known as the Gordon, draining into a huge arm of the sea—Macquarie Harbour. Snow and ice were to be met with in the highlands even at midsummer.

Few plains existed except isolated areas in the central and eastern parts and, generally speaking, the island was heavily forested. Especially along the littoral of the north-west and north-east were temperate forests of enormous eucalypts. In many places there were about 3500 trees to the acre, on average 50 feet high and 6 feet in diameter. The west and south-west was covered with bush including rainforests of impressive and fearful size and impenetrability.

The Aboriginal nomads moved over perhaps two-thirds of their island although there is evidence of their presence in winter in the most remote and inhospitable areas. Why they came into these places is a mystery; perhaps it was on an overland route, the attraction of some food supply, or a source of some material unknown to the modern observer. Perhaps certain groups were driven there by disagreements with their neighbours.

The Aboriginal people formed loose-knit groups, and there is evidence from studies of their languages that perhaps ten distinct ones existed. It appears that certain groups of these people could not understand the language of others, used different personal adornments and adopted different eating and butchering habits and practices.

The basic unit was the family or hearth-group which embodied a husband and wife (the Aborigines appear to have been monogamous), children and perhaps an aged relative or two. This hearth-group was subsumed into another larger unit or band which had a collective name and was known by that name to other Aborigines. These bands or clans numbered between seventy and eighty-five, and formed in turn twelve or thirteen larger loose groupings.

It would be an error to attach too much significance to the word 'tribe' in this context, though there may well be instructive parallels in the organization of nomadic peoples elsewhere in the world and especially to the groups of Aborigines on the mainland of Australia. In the island, Group A (whether called 'tribe' or not) could understand or come to grips with the language of its neighbouring Group B, members of which in turn could communicate in a way with Group C—but Group A could not generally understand Group C. The only time that Groups A and C came into communication appears to have been those occasions when the resource of ochre was being mined or, perhaps, when gathering

Jenny, an Aboriginal of the Port Sorell area, *c.* 1840

eggs or some such thing. In these circumstances, it may be that groups struck informal bargains, but it is not known whether such groups actually came into physical contact. It is quite possible that customs had emerged whereby certain peoples came to the ochre mines at different times.

There is some evidence of this at what Europeans came to name 'The City of Ochre', a deposit mined at Mt Gog in the north-west. In that vicinity are camp-sites quite close to each other but on different sides of the Mersey River, so that perhaps different organizations kept their distance from each other even when engaged in very similar mining activities.

But as with nearly everything of significance about the Aborigines and their culture, every answer to a question instantly raises many more questions. Quite different artefacts recovered within a few hundred yards of each other, at one mining site, suggest that the different groups of island people may well have deliberately avoided communication with each other. The problem is that when the few Europeans who did so enquired into the life of the Aborigines, the indigenous people were in a state of utter demoralization and dislocation, so that even careful observers may have noted and recorded conduct which was wildly atypical of the Aborigines when they were undisturbed.

The main groups of island people were the maritime groups who commanded lengthy seaboards and a limited hinterland (the far north-west, south-west and south-east), groups with a shore-line and a hinterland (Oyster Bay, north-east and possibly north) and groups with little or no coastline (Big (Ouse) River, north Midlands and Ben Lomond).

It must be stressed that these general areas relate to a nomadic people who were evidently constantly on the move; the geographic regions should be seen as focal points of a general territory. Yet boundaries were sometimes quite sharply demarcated, frequently being formed by a river or headland or some other natural feature. But even these might or could be crossed from time to time, probably depending on the supply of game and its pursuit. In other words, it is likely that such 'boundaries' were the actual limits of certain fauna and flora, and adopted basically in terms of food supply.

In appearance, the Aboriginal people were dark-skinned with variations from very black to 'red'. Their stature was reported by

Wooraddy, an Aboriginal of Van Diemen's Land, c. 1835

early observers to be 'average', in late-eighteenth-century European terms, and their height was about five feet in the case of women to five feet six inches for men. They had few if any clothes. Women wore a kangaroo skin arranged on the upper body and used it for carrying children and a few pieces of equipment. The men as a rule went quite naked, though both sexes wore strips of skin and necklaces of shell. People above the age of puberty were frequently marked with cicatrices: the skin was cut and then raised in patterned lines by inserting charcoal or something similar in the wound. There is some evidence that this may have been a form of group identification.

The most striking feature of the Aborigines was their scalp hair, which was distinctively tight-curled. It was frequently chopped off short by the women, some of whom had tonsured hair-styles. Men tended to plaster their scalp hair with a mixture of red ochre and grease, so that it resembled a mop or, as one observer noted wryly, the wig of a fashionable late-eighteenth-century French lady of quality. Women also adorned themselves with charcoal and ochre, to the extent of using ochre on their pubic hair. Babies were sometimes marked with ochre on their forehead and cheeks.

Mined in several locations in the island, ochre was highly prized and indeed murder was committed to get it when an exchange or form of sale went wrong. Women carried river stones to use as grinders to render down lumps of the ochre gouged from the mines with a type of chisel, and the grinding stones were frequently changed, probably by the action of fire, to form octagons and similar shapes. Some of the banana-shaped fragments discarded reveal that very narrow yet thick parts of stones were most neatly removed, but it is not clear why this was done nor why so many stones at one site were treated. It appears that the use, and perhaps preparation, of ochre may have been the sole cultural link among all the Aborigines of the island.

The diet of the people was far more various than European observers at first concluded. Nomadic life was governed by availability of food and there is no evidence that the people suffered from starvation. Observers in the eighteenth century all remarked on the good health and bright appearance of the Aborigines. Yet very little is known of their food-gathering practices in times of normality. However, the men hunted kangaroo and wallaby by cornering these animals and then bashing them to death, or by spearing. They also put down short sharpened spikes on kangaroo tracks and tied grass into loops to impede the animals when they were pursued.

Women dived for shellfish and gathered cockles and the like. Favourite spots were exploited in this way and some of the women were expert divers and swimmers. A French expedition at Adventure Bay, Bruny Island, in the late eighteenth century came up to a camp-site bestrewn with crayfish shells; the site is exploited to this day for the gathering of the crustacean.

A most interesting feature of the diet of the Aborigines is the fact that they declined to eat scaled fish. There is evidence from archaeological sites, however, that such scaled fish were consumed until about 4000 years ago. It is not clear why such a taboo—if it was one—was applied. On the face of it, the abandonment of a good food supply is astonishing because presumably the Aborigines retained the skill to catch fish if not by manufacturing hooks, then by building fish-traps or 'fisheries' to harvest at high tide the fish which haunted in-shore rocks. It may be that some powerful or influential person died as the result of choking on a fishbone, so that the word went out that all fish were now to be avoided. But this seems very odd if it pertained to all the island and all its widely different groups. On the other hand, there may have been a climatic change which rendered the capture of land food simpler than catching fish . . . but the technique of fish-traps would not have been lost, because they remained in situ once constructed. It may be that only certain areas of the island were affected but it is a fact that the Aborigines refused with horror offers of fish by maritime explorers.

Food was half-cooked over the open campfire and there is evidence that the women waited on the men. Children were disciplined by both sexes and women were secreted from some Europeans who landed prior to formal occupation of the island. A natural curiosity about the sexual characteristics of the (clothed) visitors was evinced by the Aborigines, who were puzzled by the clean-shaven Europeans and possibly concluded that all were female. They were disabused of this when one French sailor was induced to remove his clothes and then and there revealed his readiness for sexual intercourse.

The only liquid generally consumed was water, and shell containers were sometimes left beside streams to facilitate drinking. A limited supply of 'cider' from the cider gum was exploited. It was alcoholic, to a degree. The roots of certain plants were consumed, as were berries, eggs and seals.

The tool-kit of the Aborigines was a light one, as befitted a nomadic people living in a heavily-forested land which abounded with food and which was nowhere more than about sixty miles in a straight line from the sea (though sometimes hundreds of miles by Aboriginal roads). No metal is known to have been used and implements were fashioned only from wood, stone and bone. Artefacts found reveal that several varieties of scraper were devised for different purposes, and there is some tentative evidence that pieces of rock flaked off naturally by the action of frost were used as 'natural' scrapers. There is also some indication that certain objects were highly polished and perhaps carried as charms.

No tools were hafted and there is no evidence that rope or string was manufactured from hair, though sinews from kangaroo tails were employed and a type of grass made into baskets and into ropes to aid climbing trees for birds' eggs or small animals such as possums.

Cooking vessels were not employed and water was thus not boiled although containers to hold liquids were constructed from pieces of kelp. These and similar containers such as shells contained so little water that they were almost certainly used only as drinking containers and not for carrying for any serious distance. In the island that would not have been necessary as a rule, such was the rainfall and very large number of streams and lakes fed from the highlands.

Types of canoe-raft, frequently but erroneously termed 'catamarans', were made from bundles of bark or rushes, constructed in a tapered form with the ends lashed together. These craft were propelled apparently with a pole or possibly a spear, and their use was limited to short journeys to nearby off-shore islands, in clement weather. Such canoe-rafts were evidently confined to the south and south-east, thus suggesting the dominance of the environment and food supplies: Aborigines employed them to reach islands on which seals lived or, perhaps, where there were known to be very good supplies of shellfish. But as with so many other aspects of the life of the Aborigines prior to the European invasion, there is a great deal of guesswork involved in seeking to grasp their culture.

The overwhelming evidence, from objective observers, is that the people of the island were in a perfect balance and harmony with their environment. They altered it only by firing the bush. To accomplish this relationship with nature, presumably there were forms of birth-control practised but virtually nothing is known of sexual activity except a fairly conventional form of marriage: a man persisted in courting a woman until either he was successful and accepted by her and the hearth-group as a partner, or he was driven off, or he wearied of his fancied wife and went away to seek another. There is some evidence from eighteenth-century observers that men beat the women, but it is unclear. Nor is it possible to conclude anything about sexual matters from the

Paraberi, an Aboriginal of Van Diemen's Land, *c.* 1807

manner in which Aboriginal women sometimes attached themselves to Europeans, though it is possible that in some few cases
the Europeans treated them better than their own kind did.

It must be supposed that the old and severely injured were abandoned, as is the practice and indeed necessity with other nomadic
peoples, though it is interesting that a deformed man was
observed by Europeans. He may have been born that way, in
which case, why was his life spared? Or was his deformity caused
by injuries in adult life?

As a nomadic people, the Aborigines had little in the way of shelters or dwelling-places. The characteristic structure was a windbreak, built in the form of a curve from boughs and twigs and placed to obtain shelter from the prevailing winds. The use of hollow tree-stumps was also suspected, though not shown absolutely, and on the west coast quite well-constructed shelters, with a roof and possessions and decorations inside, were found. Given the severe climate of that area, such structures might have been anticipated. This may reveal that the Aborigines were not all nomadic all the time, but prepared to see out the winter in the area, perhaps subsisting upon stores? Such dwellings may have been close enough and numerous enough to warrant the name of 'village', but there is no evidence of plants being cultivated or even a primitive agricultural system developed.

The typical Aboriginal moved through the countryside equipped with spears and a fire-stick, with apparent indiscrimination setting alight virtually everything that would burn as he went along . . . but this presumably was calculated to revive the bush and thus attract animals by the appearance of fresh and tender shoots. The burnings marked out native tracks all over the island, and thus the environment was modified. After the Aborigines had been killed, an area along the Leven River in the north-west was found to be producing gum saplings in profusion where none had stood before, and this was attributed to the removal of the Aborigines.

It is now concluded that nomadic people have comparatively extensive leisure-time but little is known of how the people of the island occupied themselves when not hunting or sleeping. During the time when Europeans were with them, however, the role of story-teller and dancing appeared substantial. The story-teller spoke of historic wars or love affairs, and of the origin of his people and their environment. The Aborigines held a belief in spirits and accounted for human existence by attributing it to beings who dwelt in the heavens and who created natural features and animals as well as Aborigines. An evil spirit or force was also thought to be active, and roam among their number mysteriously and invisibly like the wind, as a sort of bogey-man. Like Europeans, they also were superstitious, and grew angry with people who cut hair perhaps or pounded ochre at the wrong time or in the wrong place, stating that such conduct would cause a storm or lead to a river coming up, and so on. Yet much of this information is derived from incidents in which it is possible the Aborigines were concealing something or, perhaps, having a joke at the expense of the credulous European.

There is no evidence that the Aborigines dwelt in sweet amity one with the other. Conflicts arose over women and equipment as elsewhere in the world and, doubtless, over many other events in their everyday life. Groups fought each other, it was stated, but the fact is that so little is known that quite contrary conclusions concerning motivation may be drawn with equal facility.

There is some evidence that herbs and plants were employed as medicine, as everywhere else; splints were made to straighten limbs broken in accidents and to facilitate the knitting of the bone. Little is known of childbirth or mortality at that time but some evidence exists relating to mortuary practices. One of the eighteenth-century French expeditions described and sketched a very elaborate tomb on Maria Island, but it is not clear whether this was a common form or not. Did eminent members of a group receive particularly special burial treatment? Among other peoples this is so, and in view of the descriptions of rather simple cremations during a later period, it may be the case. But again there is little evidence. What is certain is that how the Aborigines behaved during the course of their destruction at the hands of the Europeans may reveal little or nothing or be absolutely misleading about practices during the period prior to European conquest and the turmoil into which the Aborigines were thrown.

Petroglyphs at such places as Mt Cameron West are the only pictorial records of the Aborigines so far discovered, though it seems very unlikely that a people so fond of ochre did not daub something on the walls of over-hangs or shallow caves. If carvings of wood were created, they have not survived.

A number of Europeans sought to note vocabularies and some of the French were active in this field prior to the cultural upheaval caused by the British settlement. Yet no European mastered any of the Aboriginal languages and sought to analyse them, though G. A. Robinson in the 1830s certainly recorded thousands of words and boasted he could understand the Aborigines. His field notes do not quite bear this out but he appears certainly to have had a great ability to communicate with the people he was seeking to placate and capture. How successful he was in understanding them is uncertain and it may well be that the Aborigines were meeting him more than halfway, because they were very quick at learning English. But to Robinson is owed a great deal, as well as to N. J. B. Plomley, who first enabled Robinson's journals and vocabularies to see the light of day, thus advancing knowledge of the Aborigines by more than 100 per cent at one bound.

When all is said and done, it is likely that the Aborigines resembled their conquerors in many more ways than they differed, and were not greatly different from other nomadic peoples who lived before, during and after their time. Chaffed by Robinson for applying red ochre to their bodies on a special occasion, they snapped back, 'Why do you get dressed up for church?'

But by that time in the 1830s, the people whom the Europeans found occupying such a superbly beautiful island and moving through a landscape into which they had merged in the course of at least 12 000 years, had few enough of their number left who even dimly recalled the period of peace before the nightmare which engulfed and effectively destroyed them and their culture in one generation.

As far as is known, the first European to come to the island was Abel Jans Tasman, an employee of the Dutch East India Company. In 1642 he was sent on a voyage of exploration in search of trading opportunities and in November made a landfall on the coast of a territory he marked on his maps as Van Diemen's Land, after a high officer of the Company. A party landed, observed signs of human habitation, but sailed on to circumnavigate the undiscovered continent of Australia without actually sighting it. The Dutch turned their attentions elsewhere.

Expeditions in the eighteenth century touched at Van Diemen's Land and in 1802 Governor King at Port Jackson became nervous about the intentions of a French scientific expedition under Captain Nicolas Baudin. A good public servant, the governor concluded that his masters in the Colonial Office would not thank him for permitting foreigners to gain a foothold in an area which the British had claimed in 1770 and occupied in 1788. He proposed further British settlement to show the flag.

At the same time, reconnaissance of the new territory was being conducted by such as Matthew Flinders, and a fine body of water, thought excellent for a harbour, was found across Bass Strait from Port Dalrymple, and named Port Phillip. King and the Colonial

Office moved more or less at the same time to extend British occupation in the new land: the Governor sent Lieutenant John Bowen south to establish a presence at the Derwent and London despatched Captain David Collins to occupy Port Phillip. That was in 1803, and both expeditions employed convicts for their labour force and personnel.

When Collins arrived at Port Phillip he at once found fault with it and, perceiving that the entrance to the harbour was very difficult, decided that this was not the spot for commercial men. Other factors weighed with him, including difficulties of discipline, the hot winds, and want of fresh water. He weighed anchor and early in 1804 arrived at the Derwent, where Lieutenant Bowen had established his tiny enclave at Risdon, on the east bank.

Collins disliked this site too, and quickly moved the entire body of colonists down and across river to Sullivan's Cove, where Hobart Town was established. Shortly after Collins had thus precariously established himself in the south of Van Diemen's Land, King was active again and sent Captain William Paterson to the Tamar, to safeguard Bass Strait and ensure that any French pretensions could not be realized.

During the first years of European settlement, Van Diemen's Land settlers were several times reduced to starvation and only saved by eating native game such as emus and kangaroos, and by the fortuitous arrival of seaborne supplies. Fortunately, wheat was found to thrive in the areas around Richmond and Sorell in the south, and south-west of Launceston, and this enabled the production of all-important bread. From 1788, Norfolk Island was peopled mainly with convicts and its inhabitants were subsequently transferred during the first ten years of settlement of Van Diemen's Land. Other settlers were principally twice-convicted prisoners from Port Jackson, with some few convict ships from Britain.

During this period there developed a bandit society. It was composed of men who escaped from such penal discipline as was possible in Van Diemen's Land, and of the inhabitants on the fringes of settlement who enjoyed a life of primitive commerce. These banditti, bandits or bushrangers developed a sub-culture, perforce roamed and explored the rugged interior of the island and, continually augmented by other discontented souls from the labour gangs, effectively bade fair to threaten central government. Settlers were obliged either to abandon their holdings or to bargain with the bandits. Under Lieut.-Governor Thomas Davey, martial law was declared, but with little effect, because Governor Macquarie in Sydney angrily disapproved of his underling and because the bandits were masters of the hinterland, employing their finely-tuned commercial skills.

Michael Howe, an ex-convict, became infamous and took on many of the attributes of the bandit-hero. Impressive as were certain of their exploits—they had entire hamlets at their mercy— the bandits were finally put down when the increase of free settlement became such that they were outnumbered and out-gunned by a combination of respectable colonists and the military. The bandits moved readily through the bush at the height of their insolent power but not so freely as Aborigines, the other threat to the establishment of the colonists and their determination to exploit the island.

Because the Aborigines existed in nomadic loosely-knit social units, and were constantly on the move, it was possible for the Europeans huddled around the mouth of the Derwent and the confluence of the Esk rivers in the north, to have little communi-cation with them. Yet from earliest settlement, deaths occurred when Europeans and the invaded people clashed over food supplies such as kangaroos, and it may be that diseases introduced by the invaders also led to Aboriginal deaths without the knowl-edge of the British. There was kidnapping of Aboriginal women, especially by sealers in the north, and children were taken, and it would be foolish to suppose that the Aboriginal people meekly fell back without counter-attacks against the Europeans as the invaders ventured further inland with ever-increasing boldness.

If there was conflict and killing in these early days of settlement, how much more was there when the invaders began to establish themselves, especially after the Napoleonic wars, in the fine pastoral regions which lay between Hobart Town and Launceston. The source of conflict was very clear—both Aborigines and Europeans sought to control the same areas of land. To the Abor-igines, the land was their primary resource. They depended on its bounty for subsistence. As a hunter-gatherer people, they had come to utilize and feel part of its entire extent and resources. To the Europeans, the land was essential for business purposes. All immigrants who arrived free came to Van Diemen's Land to better themselves or at least offer their children the prospect of advancement in the colonies; that was what colonies were for. To the newcomer, the Aboriginal, who neglected to till the earth according to biblical injunction, was less than human. He had no skills, it appeared, to teach the European. He went naked, ate brutishly and, in short, was perceived as the perfect savage and without nobility of bearing. The churches did practically nothing. Certainly committees were formed by the concerned colonists and the administration suffused with the idea that something should be done to save the Aborigines from utter destruction, but little other than agonized hand-wringing was the result.

Conflict with the Aborigines was sporadic but grew in intensity to a peak about 1823–4. Typically the Aborigines sought to intimidate, wound or kill isolated shepherds and settlers advancing their sheep or cattle. A tactic was to fire the roof of a hut and then murder the occupant as he fled. Some such huts on the frontiers were fortified and equipped with loopholes.

The Europeans went on punitive expeditions and shot down Aborigines. Soldiers were equipped to remove this menace to the stock-holders of the colony; force of arms told, though it is clear that the Aborigines resisted strongly and engaged in intelligent and coherent tactics to defend themselves. It was of little avail, however, as every fresh ship discharged more free settlers anxious

Design for an early nineteenth-century banknote

to occupy land under the system of free grants. The Europeans mustered inexhaustible reserves and increasing fire-power; the Aborigines were worn down and had no reserves.

The years of this Black War were highlighted by an effort to capture the Aborigines by forming a line of soldiers and civilians across the island and 'beating' them, as it were, towards Forestier's Peninsula. This episode was much publicized but netted only two captives. Importantly, however, it brought home to the Aborigines the frightening strength of the Europeans and the forces of the army assisting them to clear the land for exploitation.

It was at this point that George Arthur, appointed governor in 1824 to take the penal colony in charge and use the labour force to promote pastoralism and the interests of Britain, approved that a patrol be sent out to bring in the remainder of the Aborigines. G. A. Robinson, a Wesleyan builder, was put in charge. In a series of extraordinarily arduous journeys, Robinson, accompanied by some Aborigines and convict servants, employed his talents to establish communication with almost all the Aboriginal people remaining in the bush and induce them to trust him. The result of this trust was the placing of the remnants of these people finally on Flinders Island, in a sort of concentration camp where most of them perished.

The decimation of the bandits and the Aborigines paved the way for the colonists to occupy all the suitable pastoral land of the island. This they largely accomplished by the mid-1830s, when the system of free land grants, encumbered merely with a nominal rent, had been removed and the sale of land substituted. Having thus occupied Van Diemen's Land, colonists new and old looked out for fresh pastures and from about 1835 began shipping their stock across Bass Strait to the new lands of the Port Phillip District of New South Wales. John Batman and John Pascoe Fawkner were active in the foundation of Melbourne, but there were many such settlers: James Whyte claimed that he took rams to the area as early as 1833.

In Van Diemen's Land the principal engine of commerce was the commissariat store. It was conducted by the government and purchased such items as meat and wheat at fixed prices in order to victual new settlers and the hordes of convict labourers. The foundation of many a Van Diemen's Land fortune was laid as a result of sales to the commissariat. By the early 1820s, production of meat gave way as a money-making speculation to the production of wool when the British industry promoted colonial wool over that hitherto got from England itself and Spain and Germany. Van Diemen's Land continued to fulfil its colonial purpose: convicts from Britain could be transported cheaply to the colony, thus ridding the metropolitan authority of trouble-makers and at the same time utilizing their muscle-power to fuel the wool industry. Van Diemen's Land became interlocked with the economy of the colonizing authority. Not only improved fleeces came to make the colony a cog in the imperial machine: whaling boomed as the island colony filled the role of place of refreshment for British whalers, and as the source of some construction of whaling vessels and equipment.

At the heart of the colonization of Van Diemen's Land by the British was the deployment of the huge labour force of convicts as virtual slave labour. The overwhelming proportion of prisoners was male, because men were stronger and far more useful than women in an age when muscle-power had not been superseded by machinery. Governor Arthur was in virtual sole charge of the outdoor penitentiary for twelve years to 1836, and brought the system of convict dispersal and management to an astonishing pitch of perfection. Prisoners were landed at an average rate of 2000 a year during this period (including about 300 females) and their exploitation was utilized by two sets of employers.

First, the government typically set convicts to work on extensive programmes of bridge-building, road-making and the like. Second, the private colonist enjoyed very cheap labour for his urban concerns or for harvesting and general rural work. Convicts were assigned. This meant that the government, in the form of the Convict Department, recorded requests for labourers and, providing the request came from a man judged to be respectable, his wants were satisfied from the convict arrivals. Labourers accommodated themselves or were housed in private or public barracks.

Discipline was progressively relaxed upon correct behaviour. Most convicts were transported for seven years (though sentences of fourteen and twenty years and life were common) and could be indulged with a ticket-of-leave after a year or so if the master recommended this and the Convict Department approved. This ticket permitted the convict to work on his or her own account on condition that regular reports were made to the police. If the prisoner continued steady, the sentence might be waived and a free or conditional pardon issued. The free pardon, presented only for outstanding public service, restored the convict to the privileges of a British citizen. A conditional pardon also similarly restored the prisoners but on condition they not return to Britain. In this way, some convicts rapidly were rehabilitated and not infrequently became wealthy if not respectable in the eyes of the 'pure merino' settler.

Misconduct earned punishment. This varied from chastisement to execution and in between was a kaleidoscopic variety of experiences and punitive measures. Female convicts were more difficult to control in terms of punishment. In the early days of settlement they were certainly flogged on the bare back, had their scalp hair shorn off and were subjected to other special punishments. Normally women were lodged in gaol, however, when guilty of misconduct, and the Female Factory at Hobart Town was used as a lying-in hospital.

Female convicts were sexually exploited though it should be noted that governors such as George Arthur went to considerable lengths to minimize this exploitation by enquiring very closely into the moral character of free settlers who applied for female servants, and seeking to assign women prisoners only to respectable families.

When the Commissioner of Enquiry, J. T. Bigge, recommended to the British government in the early 1820s that the colonies be organized so as more effectively to exploit the convict labour force poured in, it became necessary to construct places of secondary punishment. The principal one of these was opened in 1821 at Macquarie Harbour, having earlier been promoted by Lieut.-Governor Sorell. There the conditions of labour were as severe as the human frame would stand; the men were employed principally in cutting down the Huon pine logs which grew in such profusion to the water's edge along the Gordon River. Desperate men committed desperate deeds at Sarah Island, the convict station. Some coolly murdered in order to get a 'slant', which was slang for a journey back to Hobart Town for trial and execution, but the actual proportion of convicts who were employed at Macquarie Harbour was small.

In 1830 a new settlement was formed at Port Arthur, where the

Map of Van Diemen's Land, 1824

principal work was timber-felling and milling, and coal-mining. On a tip of land adjacent to the main settlement was established a boys' prison known as Point Puer, an enlightened experiment for its time. Escape from the settlements at Port Arthur was virtually impossible because dogs were tied up across Eaglehawk Neck, the very narrow strip which was sole entry and exit by land to and from the Peninsula.

Port Arthur was chosen with care as a place of secondary punishment by virtue of its isolation from the settled areas of Van Diemen's Land and for the prospect of employing convicts fruitfully while they underwent severe discipline. Certainly it was not a bed of roses, but it came to gain a much worse reputation than it deserved.

Depicted as a hell on earth, it was spoken of in the same breath as Macquarie Harbour and Norfolk Island, places where dramatic highlights were also characterized as the norm. This was understandable, up to a point, especially when in the 1850s and 1860s men released from Port Arthur committed offences which drew attention to their origin; the evil reputation of the place was further stressed as colonists sought to distance themselves from their convict past and desperately seek respectability.

Further images were shaped not least by Marcus Clarke's gothic novel *For the Term of his Natural Life*, a work of fiction published first as *His Natural Life* in 1874 and going into many editions. It was lent verisimilitude by the list of official documentary sources attached to it. The conduct of Port Arthur as a penal establishment came to be judged by the enlightened standards of penology belonging to the later nineteenth and the twentieth centuries. A 'museum' display enriched by the exhibition of leg-irons and other such relics was calculated to send a thrill of horror through the observer and implant a conviction that the bad old days were indeed appalling.

Although a sentence to Port Arthur was initially reserved for the dyed-in-the-wool offender and those found guilty of the most grave criminal offences or persistent bad conduct, it should be stressed that the standards of the time were very different from those of a later period and that some inmates of Port Arthur or Point Puer turned out to be the founders of respectable Tasmanian families.

Van Diemen's Land was an extremely violent society, comprising as it did many of the desperate men who had emerged from the social dislocation produced as the Industrial Revolution gathered pace. Not only was bloody flagellation of convicts very common, because it was a cheap and efficient method of punishment which did not lead to the victim being absent from work very long, but so also was execution. Public hangings were conducted at a frequency which rid the colony of malefactors very rapidly in the early years of Arthur's administration. The ritual of executions was ever to be observed, when the doomed victims dressed elaborately in order to be delivered into eternity. The press exhorted its readers to take notice of such events and tremble. The government assisted in brutalization of the people by rewarding citizens who brought in the head of a bandit. Men on the run from Arthur's convict labour gangs lunged about the colony, their conduct varying from mocking good manners to sudden and ghastly murders. The Wesleyan missionaries imported by the authorities blanched at what they saw and concluded that they could never labour too long in such a barbarous society.

At the centre of Van Diemen's Land was the humourless person of Governor Arthur. He learnt well the skills of colonial administration in British Honduras and was appointed governor of the island colony after listing his main achievements and cultivating patrons in London. Arthur was a proconsul of the first order and the subject of countless attempts at character assassination by the touchy settlers of Van Diemen's Land. The Colonial Office continued to control the development of the colony and Arthur was ever conscious of his role as chief executive, chief gaoler and guardian of morality. He had been sent to Van Diemen's Land to hold in check the criminality of the Empire and for his twelve years in office discharged that function with a skill as amazing as it was comprehensive.

In 1825 Van Diemen's Land was administratively detached from New South Wales and equipped with its own judicial establishments and Legislative Council. During the course of his administration, Arthur led his Council by the nose because he mastered all aspects of administration, because he possessed the power to appoint convict labour, and because he presided over an economic boom. Yet he was loathed by many colonists because he checked them by here withdrawing a name from the Commission of the Peace, and there pressing a man to resign.

Despite these onsets by disaffected colonists who found they could not make a fortune if they offended the evangelical values of Arthur, the governor met the exacting requirements of the

Colonial Office. In an age when civil servants expected to advance their interests by diligent embezzlement, Arthur came down hard on the many incompetents with whom he was surrounded as the result of patronage by politically effective gentlemen in England. Treasury officials were revealed to be innumerate, clerks virtually illiterate, customs officers hand-in-glove with the merchants from whom they were expected to extract taxes. Arthur entrapped them by conducting simultaneous audits of related account books and treasury chests, intercepted mail to discredit them in Britain, was unremitting in drawing the attention of the Colonial Office to the sexual behaviour of some, and promoted those whom he thought he could trust.

During his regime the press of Van Diemen's Land flourished as if in a hot-house, and despite the governor's determined attempts to control their outpourings by censorship, the newspapers agitated for a legislative assembly and especially for trial by jury. In 1828, Britain enlarged the size of the Legislative Council and the boon of trial by jury in certain cases came to be vouchsafed, though Arthur feared the worst.

He need not have worried unduly because those elements of the colonial population who fancied themselves as legislators and tribunes of the people did not dream of placing any political control in the hands of the great unwashed. British government and prominent colonists shared a commonality of interests in seeking to keep effective power in the right hands. The colonists and the British colonizing authority drew closer together as the former began to achieve the social status and wealth they so neurotically sought.

Freed of the threat of bandits and Aborigines, the colonists of Van Diemen's Land began to develop a cultural style. At the top, the wealthy and educated promoted schools and subsidized them and their religion, and the state did the same. Holidays celebrated British events such as the King's birthday, St George's Day, and the Christian festivals. Harvest customs were transferred to the antipodes, cricket was played and there were always horse races and hunting. Pugilists had purses wagered on them as they came up to scratch for round after round, and in the main centres theatrical entertainments flourished. In private, artistic colonists met to discuss their painting and sketches. Lawyers and solicitors abounded because the people were naturally litigious and could

George Arthur, Governor of Van Diemen's Land 1824–36

afford to take each other to court. Religion remained not much more than a form with many nominal Anglicans, though the Wesleyans perceived the people to be in a fallen state, preached with evangelical fervour and were caught up in religious revivals from time to time. The strength of the Catholic church was not substantial until Irish convicts came to be transported in large numbers from 1840s, but free persons came to the colony in increasing numbers in the 1830s.

By the end of Arthur's administration in 1836, the total population of the colony was 43 000, of whom 24 000 were 'free' (14 000 males and 10 000 females), and 19 000 convicts (17 000 males and 2000 females). About 11 000 free persons arrived in the 1830s. Some 75 per cent of the people of Van Diemen's Land were convicts, had been convicts or were of convict ancestry.

2

Imitation

On a spring morning in 1836, Governor George Arthur made his way from Government House down to the wharf, weeping bitterly and supported by Chief Justice Pedder. Usually most undemonstrative, he now revealed his sorrow at departing from the colony over which he had reigned for so long, and made way for a new chief executive of the world's most notorious penal colony.

This was Sir John Franklin, the Polar hero. Although of undoubted personal courage, the new man was inexperienced in administration of colonies, especially one as turbulent as Van Diemen's Land. He inherited Arthur's smooth-running government and also that governor's smooth lieutenants, John Montagu and Matthew Forster, Colonial Secretary and Chief Police Magistrate respectively.

At the beginning, the convict system went on as before. Prisoners continued to dominate expenditure and general business, although the free immigrants and those born within the colony began to reduce the impact of convictism in numerical terms. Yet prisoners remained nearly 40 per cent of the total population in 1840.

Franklin's government was soon presented with an enormous administrative problem when, from 1840, all convicts sentenced to transportation in Britain were forwarded to Van Diemen's Land because transportation to New South Wales ceased. This flood coincided unfortunately with economic depression in the early 1840s and at the same time the governor's competence came under attack. His principal difficulties, however, lay in other quarters.

Franklin was accompanied by his energetic wife, Lady Jane, and neither of them cared for the day-to-day business of conducting a penal colony. Rather they sought contact with savants and

25

distinguished travellers who ventured with curiosity to the island colony. The Franklins relished the work involved in promoting education and religion and generally behaved as high-minded lord and lady of a reforming manor. The Hobart Town regatta became a regular feature of their patronage, a learned society was formed by their encouragement of science, and the *Tasmanian Journal of Natural Science* was founded. Franklin enjoyed the company of such as Ronald Campbell Gunn, the botanist and public servant whose work was to be of such importance in the acceptance of Darwin's theory of evolution.

The governor was most interested in forwarding primary education and under the guidance of Britain, a Board of Education was established in 1839 to supervise a system of non-denominational schooling. It did not and could not, however, attract the best teachers on the basis of pupils' fees and, in addition, the Church of England raised the most grave objections to a scheme in which the precepts of religious beliefs were not to

Convict chain gang, *c.* 1852

be an integral part of the school syllabus, but an addition as it were.

In the field of religion, too, state aid was offered from 1838 towards stipends and costs of church building but again there arose opposition from such as the Church of England on the grounds that if it were admitted that religious truth was attainable by more than one religion, this would lead to the destruction of them all. Less acrimonious was the establishment of the Hutchins School in Hobart Town and a Grammar School at Launceston, and the appointment of the first Anglican bishop in the person of F. R. Nixon was welcomed as an indication of the importance of Van Diemen's Land.

More humble folk began to embrace that peculiarly colonial form of culture which came to be known as 'moral enlightenment'. It was a secular belief with a half-baked ideology which stressed utility, earnestness and abstinence from intoxicating drinks. It frowned upon displays of enthusiasm, embodied a kill-joy mentality and elevated the virtues of the semi-literate. It went great guns in a burgeoning colonial setting where ambitious working people formed the prospectively pretentious.

An associated movement was that of Mechanics' Institutes, where the respectable working man might read newspapers and attend improving lectures. It was as if in Van Diemen's Land a fresh form of religious belief was being shaped while the principal churches faltered because they could seldom meet the expectations and needs of a colonial population which lacked a sense of history. In this atmosphere Wesleyanism flourished.

Franklin seldom satisfied the mandarins of Downing Street: he never lived up to the expectations of such as John Montagu, and became the victim of terrorism by rumour, his own bluff incompetence, the malevolence of men who respected strength and authority rather than flexibility and liberalism, and the ill-advised intervention of the governor's wife in official transactions. The Franklins, admirable and cultivated, were the wrong people in the wrong place at the wrong time. The governor vainly looked out for an indication of support from the Colonial Office. He received none and was obliged to resign in 1843. Returning to the sea, he disappeared while in search of the north-west passage.

His replacement was Sir John Eardley Eardley-Wilmot, a country gentlemen from Warwickshire with an interest in crime.

He was offered an opportunity unparalleled in the history of the world to satisfy his curiosity. A new convict system called probation was now in full swing, requiring that prisoners be housed in camps where they should be disciplined and employed with a view to passing through various stages of rehabilitation, and be hired out from depots established for the purpose. Because of the huge numbers transported, the depression of the period and the slackening in demand for convict labour, this system of transportation began to come under heavy criticism. Not surprisingly the subject of money lay at the heart of this: some colonists objected to paying, through taxes, portion of the costs of administering gaols and police. Cost-benefit analysis was reinforced by moral considerations as an element of the colonial population began drawing attention to sexual aberrations said to be practised with impunity in the ranks of the convict labour force. Eardley-Wilmot's Legislative Council walked out on him concerning the voting of money for the convict system and the governor of Van Diemen's Land came under more unfavourable notice from the Colonial Office when he quarrelled with the Bishop of Tasmania, Nixon.

The principal point at issue concerned a conflict between church and state on the question of appointment and control of chaplains to the convict department of government. On other matters also the administration of a British colony entrusted temporarily to Eardley-Wilmot was judged less than satisfactory by his metropolitan masters. W. E. Gladstone, a new Secretary of State, objected that the education of the rising generation is not affected sufficiently by the beliefs of the Church of England, and blamed the governor for this deficiency. More seriously, the Secretary of State grew alarmed at the meagre reports reaching him concerning what he chose to describe as the moral state of the convicts.

Egged on by James Stephen, principal under-secretary, Gladstone began to be impressed with the lack of commitment exhibited by the governor in this important particular. Bishop Nixon's allies in England lost no opportunity to place the conduct of the governor in an unfavourable light and to spread stealthy rumours of improper conduct at Government House. Preparing to find a reason for dismissing Eardley-Wilmot, the Colonial Office began keeping a record of his shortcomings so that they could muster evidence when the governor, as they began to close

Port Arthur penal settlement, *c.* 1852

in on him, finally received the fatal message. Eardley-Wilmot was
said to enjoy the company of young women and it was further
put about that he brought female convicts into Government House
for a lewd entertainment. Certainly the governor's wife had not
accompanied him to Van Diemen's Land and thus such rumours
were permitted to gather strength. Finally, in 1847 Gladstone
penned a lethal despatch of official recall and accompanied it with
another 'private' document which spoke darkly of rumours associated with the governor of the island colony.

Eardley-Wilmot was incredulous, startled and finally furious at
this ignominious end to his gubernatorial career. Mustering such
political support as he could, the governor fought back but
Gladstone was shortly removed from the Colonial Office on his
way to higher things and avoided having to justify the dismissal.
The hapless governor lingered at Van Diemen's Land, awaiting
his successor, and died a few days after the arrival of Sir William
Denison. The colonists concluded that he had perished of a broken
heart and ill-treatment at the hands of Downing Street

bureaucrats, and erected a grand mausoleum for the purpose of containing the late governor's mortal remains. At the funeral, Van Diemen's Land clerics behaved with characteristic rivalry when the Catholic and Anglican clergy sought to glide in front of each other in a subtle struggle for precedence in the melancholy procession.

The colonists' daring but confident behaviour reflected the triumph of the successful colonist; by now the gentry had succeeded in forming a coherent class which appeared to place its impress on the society in a permanent manner. The triumph of the wool industry strengthened their confidence and increased their opulence, and there was constructed in the wool country which stretched between Hobart Town and Launceston, with spurs to the west and east, a number of colonial mansions which were brilliant examples of the architects' skill. Cool, confident and colonial Georgian, they were epitomized by the country seats of the Archer family—the brothers Thomas, Joseph, William, and Edward, and their father. The homesteads they built on the basis of free land grants, free labour and shrewdness were among the finest in the booming colony. The Archers had a crested family vault in the cemetery of Christ Church, Longford. They also had 'Panshanger', built by Joseph Archer on a knoll near the Lake River adjoining his brother Thomas's estate. Breathtakingly beautiful, it summed up to perfection the triumph of the gentry of Van Diemen's Land.

At the other extreme of colonial existence were the inarticulate semi-slave labourers, usually with tickets-of-leave, dwelling in slab huts and being paid by the truck system, in kind and not in money. The exploiters rewarded such workers in tea and sugar and made wood and water available to them, which the poor durst not refuse.

A step above these victims of colonialism were such as the Huon settlers. Their only communication with the outside world was by ship to Hobart Town. Mainly labourers, ex-convicts and ticket-of-leave men, they had only a few pounds of capital at the most and aimed to subsist until they could clear enough land to produce some surplus. Such settlers scrubbed the land, felled the small trees and cleared the undergrowth during first years of occupation of the bush. The numerous big trees were ring-barked and left to die. The next stage was logging up, in which bullock teams and hand labour were used to drag logs and branches into heaps for late autumn burning. This continued the second year and with the smaller stumps and roots grubbed out, an effort was made to cultivate a crop, perforce planted between the stumps and standing ring-barked trees.

During this stage of extremely hard work, muscle-power was clearly king of the economy but there was some compensation in the first crops from a rich and virgin soil. Most settlers aimed to clear about ten to fifteen acres to support themselves and their families but in the early stages they were content with a few acres on which to erect a primitive homestead and plant a kitchen garden.

The Huon settler's first house was usually a most primitive affair of two slab-walled rooms roofed with sheets of bark held on by logs and stones. The chimney was frequently made of wood lined with mud, the whole surmounted by an old cask which served as a chimney pot.

But not all Van Diemen's Land was as heavily timbered as the Huon when it was being laboriously settled in the era before the great Victorian gold rushes. In other areas the production of wheat remained important. Threshing-machines were employed certainly by 1827; they were equipped with a mechanism for cleaning the grain and were commonly hired out. Reapers were in use before 1845 and in that year a Van Diemen's Land variation of the stripper was in operation and reported to reap twenty acres a day with two horses. Most farmers, however, reaped and threshed by hand in the early 1840s, hitting the grain with a flail or treading it out by foot. Advertisements for farm machinery usually mentioned only ploughs, harrows, chains and carts, with an occasional thresher or winnower, in 1842.

When by his death Sir John Eardley Eardley-Wilmot ceased to trouble the Colonial Office and its moralists any longer, the policy-makers of Downing Street began to face a mounting barrage of pleas, arguments, abuse and threats from Van Diemen's Land on the subject of transportation of convicts. Sir William Denison arrived to discover that the matter of paying for the costs of police and gaols continued to obsess the local politically effective, some of whom also now objected to the continuation of any transportation.

There came to be formed the Anti-Transportation League, its moral impulse largely derived from northern Nonconformists

Poster opposing the transportation of convicts, 1850

such as the Reverend John West. Its stern public voice was the Launceston *Examiner* and Denison found himself beset as he attempted to implement British policy and continue the probation system. With the lifting of the economic depression by the mid-1840s, those who opposed transportation were able to do so on the grounds that it was morally wicked and driving the respectable to Port Phillip. As a great deal of scary evidence was adduced, once again eloquence was shown not necessarily to be the friend of truth. The Colonial Office heard of cannibalism and unnatural practices indulged in upon a scale not dreamt of by the readers of Catullus; the London *Times* took up the cudgels through the person of Robert Lowe, late of New South Wales and dedicated to attacking the British administration; Denison was the subject of intense propaganda by the League, although throughout he retained the confidence of the colony's masters in London.

In 1851, the Legislative Council, though still retaining an official appointed component, was enlarged and liberalized. Those elected, on a very high property qualification, were anti-transportationist to a man, and the legislators began to prepare to take over the government and draw up a constitution to satisfy

London. While the members of the Council, aided by executive officers of government and the thoughts of Denison, laboured to produce a written basis for government, gold was being found in Victoria.

Large-scale emigration set in from Van Diemen's Land to Port Phillip and inflation caused the costs of convict administration to jump sensationally. Transportation of convicts came to an end when the last convict vessel docked at Hobart Town on 26 May 1853, and the colony gave itself up to celebration and marked the end of a chapter by renaming the island Tasmania, to commemorate the discoverer.

Tasmania yet remained a colony in all respects, as did the other provinces of Britain in Australia. The people were fanatically loyal to the Crown and Britain and outdid themselves in patriotism during the Crimean War, donating huge sums of money to the imperial cause and emotionally reacting to the course of events. Side by side with this high loyalty was a great pride in the beauty of the island. Ashamed of its violent, convulsive and most unrespectable past, and conscious of their isolation out on the very edge of the Empire, the people fostered imperial sentiment to interlock with their economic dependence on Britain and cultural unity with it. The green appearance of the colony, in contrast to the summer scorching administered to the mainland colonies, induced the inhabitants of Tasmania to perceive their colonial home as a little England.

Hedge-rows were smiled upon as a reminder of a Merrie England few if any of them had really ever known, the destruction of the native flora and fauna and its replacement by exotics went on apace, a fact which added to the picture of colonists being merely transplanted Britons. The power and strength of the Church of England and the appointment of bishops and governors from England, speaking correctly and not through the colonial nose, reinforced the humble relationship of the colony to the imperial authority. 'Home' was Britain. The literate drew cultural sustenance from the works of Dickens, Thackeray and Borrow, and followed news from 'Home' with nostalgic interest. The Great Exhibition of 1851 was viewed with intense satisfaction. The island took pride in being an antipodean sanatorium and sanctuary for those pillars of the Empire who lived or fought in India, and were obliged to seek rest and recreation leave in the temperate

Tasmanian colonists in their finery

climes of lovely Tasmania before returning to the jewel in the crown. The private school system was slavishly modelled upon that of England and the public state schools inculcated a British syllabus.

The development of a middle class was checked as the population increase slowed down with the end of transportation and the superior attractions of Victoria, equipped as it was with goldfields and unlimited opportunities for the resourceful and the unscrupulous, many of whom had received an excellent grounding in Van Diemen's Land.

The triumph of the gentry and of British political forms could not have been more complete when the Constitution Act of 1855 was passed by the British government. This represented the result of no serious struggle for responsible government, because both the metropolitan colonizing authority and the gentry were agreed that political power should be transferred merely from one set of rulers to another. The Legislative Council, the House of Assembly and the Crown (in the person of the governor as Her Majesty's representative) constituted the classical trinity of political sovereignty in Tasmania as in the other colonies, with the salaries of the judiciary and civil service guaranteed. Only one or two radical men considered that government should be other than in the hands of the class equipped to govern.

The Legislative Council was retained, with power to block any legislation submitted to it by the House of Assembly. Further, the council was to be elected on a very high property qualification and seat only gentlemen who had independent means. It would be difficult to imagine a more elite body. On the other hand, the illusion of a people's government was fostered by devising a people's House which had a basic franchise of £10 householders. Even this liberal arrangement debarred many adult males from voting, and the distribution and structure of population made certain that rural districts were able to exert a majority opinion over the urban centres of Hobart Town and Launceston.

Such was the importance of the pattern set in the early proceedings of elections and parliaments in the colony that close attention must be paid to early issues and preoccupations, assumptions and expectations of the people and their representatives, and the events of these first years. Government principally by a chief executive appointed from the Colonial Office and responsible to London was not completely swept away in the mid-1850s but there was to be no opportunity to cast all blame for colonial misfortunes on the governor and his political masters at home.

There was called into existence in 1855 a Constitution Act which carefully ensured that there should be government by the propertied class, and on 1 May Her Majesty the Queen assented to legislation which established a parliament for her colony of Tasmania. There was to be an election for the House of Assembly every three years but members of the Legislative Council retired on a system of rotation, so that it could not be dissolved and was in fact in continuous existence. This provision was to prove a matter of the utmost significance.

Elections for the parliament were spread over a period of three weeks or a month. This permitted defeated candidates to try for election again, and also was designed to allow persons who owned property in more than one constituency to vote several times. However, even occasional coincidence of elections did not prevent plural voting. In 1861, for example, a hard-riding James Gibson in the morning first thing recorded his vote at Avoca for the Fingal seat in the House and in the afternoon voted at Deloraine for the electorate there, having travelled across country on horseback. Again, during another election, the *Emu* was chartered to carry up to New Norfolk such of W. S. Sharland's supporters as were resident in Hobart Town.

In 1857 the northern electorates (north of and including Camp-bell Town) had a total population of about 32 000 persons, and the southern ones 49 000. By 1870, however, the north had almost overtaken the south in terms of population: 50 000 to 53 000. In demographic terms the feature of the period was the marked increase of population in the north. Hobart Town's population increased by less than 1000 to 19 500 in the period to 1870 whereas Launceston advanced from 8000 to 11 000. This palpable change in the centre of population gravity was reflected in continual fric-tion between the interests of Launceston and the capital, compli-cated by the development of a new regional interest along the north-west and, up to a point, in the north-east. The very marked regional loyalties in the colony were reinforced greatly by the circulation of newspapers: the boundary between north and south was marked in part by the areas where the Launceston *Examiner* and Hobart Town *Mercury* were read, which coincided with business interests. Hobart always had what Launceston and the north regarded as an unfair edge because the capital was the seat of government and the main government departments, and because it possessed a marvellous harbour and facilities for seaborne trade.

Despite the colonists' delight at the prospect of living in a colony with self-government, the first such election in 1856 revealed a remarkable apathy in terms of electioneering, because only fourteen of the thirty seats (nearly all in or near Hobart Town or Launceston) were contested. The seat of Norfolk Plains (Longford) was to have had a second candidate, but at the eleventh hour he walked away across the common and lay concealed in a ditch all day.

Thus was the boon of self-government ushered in—and out, because in its first eight months' enjoyment of the novelty, the colony had no fewer than four ministries. The first premier was the Launceston member, W. T. N. Champ, with T. D. Chapman as colonial treasurer and Francis Smith as attorney-general. This administration collapsed after four months when, faced with a large deficit in estimated revenue, attributed without evidence to long years of irresponsible rule and extravagant expenditure, it imposed additional customs duties on such items as food and clothing, postage, shipping, tobacco, tea and sugar in an attempt to meet a budget deficiency. In an interesting move, Chapman proceeded to implement the provisions of this before the Legislative Council passed judgement on the bill. At a subsequent conference between the houses, no conclusion was reached on the power of the Council and, thus confirmed and encouraged, that body proceeded for many years to amend bills in season and out.

The triumph of the Council was not generally noticed as upwards of 5000 people attended a meeting of protest at the New Market in Hobart Town against the proposed duties, and noted that the proposed tax was oppressive on the industrial classes, permitted the landed gentry and men of capital to evade a just share of the burden of government, that smuggling and illicit distillation would flourish, and that the principles of free trade were being attacked. Petitions were got up, the one at Hobart Town said to be thirty-eight yards long. The House reassembled after an adjournment and in February 1857 the ministry was defeated.

Champ's administration was succeeded by that of T. G. Gregson, who promptly produced a memorandum. The year's deficit was of the order of £76 000, announced this document, and it went on to adumbrate details of land sales, reduction of salaries and the floating of a credit vote. This was refused by the House and stirring scenes followed. Gregson had a reputation for turbulence and eccentricity, and possessed a fatal genius for antagonizing people. The principal features of his political career were said to be a few speeches on popular topics of the day, two or three discreditable attempts at horse-whipping people (including the nephew of Governor Arthur—but after Arthur had sailed for England), and a duel. Against this ideological background, in the House he indulged in offensive personal vituperation, sought to revive against political opponents the indiscretions of a quarter of a century earlier, and made faces.

The end came for the premier when in March he asked the House to sanction the proposed loan. This was opposed by Chapman whereupon Gregson made a splendidly insulting speech in which he accused Chapman of coming out to Van Diemen's Land as a steward on a ship. There was fearful excitement in the public gallery.

Gregson was succeeded by W. P. Weston, whose administration fell back on retrenchment, land sales and some extra duties on certain imported goods. Then Francis Smith became premier in a reshuffle and political peace settled over the land.

The number of adult males declined and there were reductions in import and export figures. The *Daily News*, sole liberal voice in the colonial wilderness, concluded gloomily that there was little chance of the government actually doing anything for the benefit of the industrial classes because the majority of the members of parliament remained largely and deeply concerned with the maintenance of the status quo.

The colony exhibited symptoms of collapse. A joint parliamentary committee appointed to enquire into the tariff lapsed for want of a quorum, expansion of the franchise was spoken of as one of the most objectionable features of American republicanism, and had it not been for observations about the chances of gold being found, the governor's speech on the opening of the fifth session of parliament in August 1859 would have been limited to the subjects of the eradication of thistles and the introduction of salmon.

During the period of office of the first parliament of Tasmania, however, there emerged an issue which was to trouble every ministry. This concerned the introduction of railways. The steam, as it were, for this manifestation of the Industrial Revolution came especially from the north of Tasmania and took the form of agitation for a line of rail from Launceston to Deloraine across a level and very fertile countryside. In July 1858 a parliamentary committee looked into the matter and ten months later a British firm indicated its willingness to lay down forty miles of track. In 1861 the government made a fateful decision when it agreed to bear the cost of survey and plans, provided that the local people raised money for building the line.

But at that point, the House was dissolved and the second of the colony's elections ordered. No startling or new political issues appeared on the horizon, the legislature and government being dominated and dictated to by the Chamber of Commerce. This body was composed exclusively of importers and commission agents, it was said, and it was quite hopeless to expect revision of the tariff because this would involve a collision with those powerful camarillas.

Most of the candidates in 1861 were landed proprietors, merchants and lawyers. There was an element of mild excitement in that five men stood for Hobart Town on a Protection ticket. Fifty-six men offered themselves for re-election, and eleven had a walk–over; fifteen men were newcomers to the House. Apart from the general question of how to raise money, the chief issue was protection for local industry, urged by a section of the press, but the new House of Assembly gave no sign that it would differ in any serious way from the old one. All in all, the election was

Aspects of colonialism, 1901

favourable to the ministry and northern free trade influences. Though Chapman was rejected in Hobart Town, he got in for the down-river constituency of Queenborough and shortly became premier.

The election having been concluded, the Legislative Council now felt the necessity to stir itself by adopting a role which might be termed either public-spirited or intransigent—it refused to accept the next appropriation bill until the colonial treasurer had explained to the Council's satisfaction how he intended to raise the necessary funds. In response, F. M. Innes announced that because he estimated a deficit of £30 000, he proposed a further issue of debentures, together with ad valorem duties. The Council, possibly victim of some lapse of attention, passed these measures and then angrily carried a vote of no confidence on the question of the ad valorem duties which it had so recently approved. When the House disregarded this, the Council characteristically refused to proceed with any business at all and directed the Governor to dismiss the ministry.

The tariff aroused great hostility from the mercantile interests and from sections of the people but, the government persisting, the Council in September 1862 rejected Supply and Chapman was defeated on the floor of the House. The Legislative Council had struck again although the government would be obliged to decide between ad valorem duties and direct taxation—or bankruptcy.

The election of 1862 was about confidence in the ministry and its financial policy, so Chapman's administration was decisively defeated. When parliament reassembled early in 1863, leadership of the government was vested in C. J. Whyte, member for Pembroke in the Legislative Council, and hailed as leader of a 'liberal' party. The policy of the new men turned out to be further retrenchment, readjustment of taxation and the institution of public works, but a Royal Commission appointed to enquire into the public service inconveniently found that retrenchment had been carried to its limit by the preceding government. Some other means of increasing revenue without upsetting anyone of importance had therefore to be found. This was difficult and an attempt to compel local areas to pay for roads and education was hastily withdrawn.

More interest was shown in the approach of the railway era. By early 1862 a survey of railway between Launceston and Deloraine had been conducted by W. T. Doyne, the government surveyor, and it was estimated that £365 000 would be needed to cover costs of building the line. Great enthusiasm in the north was reported, especially among individuals whose land values would be enhanced. One of the most active railway men was Sir Richard Dry and he stated that £400 000 was the maximum required for a railway. It was proposed to secure this amount by asking the government to authorize the issue of debentures with a guarantee of the interest. Inhabitants of the railway district were to be asked to re-guarantee to the government half of that interest, assured by an assessment on their land. In mid-1863 there was recommended the establishment of a board of railway commissioners to usher in the railway age . . . but the Legislative Council rejected this and a fresh body was appointed to look into the practicability of a line between Launceston and Hobart Town.

Northern members were furious, and blamed W. R. Allison and what the *Examiner* termed his characteristic absurdity. But northern plans went ahead anyway and a Northern Railway League was inaugurated at a public meeting in September 1863 as the climax to a full day of festivities in Launceston. Most northern members of parliament were in the League, with Dry as chairman and Henry Dowling secretary.

At the same time, however, a main line committee was formed to canvass subscriptions for a railway between Hobart Town and the north; further to complicate matters, a company was established to build a line from Deloraine on to the Mersey; and yet another body, called the Direct Western Railway Company, was said to be promoting a line in order to undermine the League. The enterprise of the north began to be feared and southern citizens contemplated now with horror the transfer of the capital of Tasmania from the broad and beautiful estuary of the Derwent to the narrow and tortuous mudflats of the Tamar.

As a result of negotiations between Dry and the colonial secretary there finally emerged an agreement by which the government was to authorize the formation of a Launceston–Deloraine railway company, and guarantee the issue of railway bonds, with the government to have a lien on the railway plant and revenue, with power to levy a rate on the railway district for any deficiency. Agreement to the whole proposal was reached at a public meeting of the League at which landholders were told they would be polled to determine their willingness to be subjected to a rate if necessary. The quid pro quo for parliamentary agreement to this was apparently the passage of a bill authorizing the expenditure of £106 000 on public works.

Meanwhile the construction of a line from Deloraine to the Mersey had begun, the company undertaking the work in return for grants of land of one mile depth on either side of the railway. In the south the main line had not advanced beyond the formation of a railway progress association and in the north a railway poll was conducted, 2238 landholders favouring the measure and only 564 opposing it. The *Examiner* printed a comprehensive account of the day's voting on blue paper, blue being the colour of the League's flag.

In an attempt to promote further public works, and get the colony on the move, the Whyte government then adopted the recommendations of a select committee on the matter, but the Legislative Council instantly threw out the bill. In these circumstances, the government decided on a bold and desperate venture: in July 1865, the governor informed a horrified gentry that his government had now determined to free the port of Hobart Town, to remove duties from everything except beer, spirits and tobacco, and to substitute a property and income tax of 1s. in the pound (5 per cent) on all incomes over £80 a year. Such a programme, concluded the treasurer sunnily, would not only place the revenue of Tasmania on a sure and certain foundation but would invite trade, commerce and population, and give a healthy stimulus to industry.

It was all too much. What will our friends in England think of us! cried the *Mercury*. Public meetings sprang into life up country to protest, and it was predicted that landholders would sell out rather than pay up. In the House, Meredith's proposal was quickly destroyed, though the final lethal motion opposing his plans was carried by only one vote finally. In September 1866 the third parliament of Tasmania was dissolved, and members once more went to the country to present electors with a choice between retrenchment (which was no longer possible) and further orthodox taxation (which was also no longer possible). It remained only for the power of prayer to be called up.

The years 1865 and 1866 were very bad ones for Tasmania economically for at only one other time had revenue been lower than it was in 1866; coin held in the banks was never less; the value of exports was lower than in any other year, and imports were only half the value recorded in 1855. On all sides it was agreed that the tax proposal was the issue to be decided at the polls. Even the question of whether or not the government should subsidize the building of the western railway dropped out of sight in relation to the competition of an income tax.

The election in Hobart Town was rowdy and candidates were handled roughly: W. L. Crowther had no sooner commenced a speech than a man stood up at the bottom of the platform, demanded payment of an account and then threw an egg; Chapman was also the target for a man throwing eggs, which missed, at which Mr Chapman asked if that was an Englishman.

As in Hobart Town, so in Launceston government candidates were defeated at the hands of H. E. Lette, J. Crookes and J. Scott who were supported by the Railway League, which thus delivered them the seats. Significantly, Charles Meredith, the Treasurer who had promoted the proposed tax, was himself defeated in Glamorgan by his brother John, although anti-government voters going to the electorate were nobbled when some ruffians took the wheels off their dogcart and the nuts off the bolts. Charles Meredith did however finally secure a seat for Kingborough.

F. M. Innes spoke solemnly of the natural subordination of one class to another, and enough people believed that the government's proposals would lead only to equality of misery. As the sole candidate for New Norfolk, W. S. Sharland, stated in an injured tone, he disapproved of class legislation such as the direct tax and thought it morally wrong to set gentlemen against poor men.

A ministry led by Sir Richard Dry came into office in November 1866 with Chapman as colonial treasurer and W. L. Dobson as attorney-general. It was supposed to undertake sweeping retrenchment; it withdrew £20 000 of grants-in-aid to municipalities, and within a month fell back on the issue of debentures to meet the interest about to fall due on all the other debentures issued by previous administrations.

While the railway issue embittered relations between north and south, the government did succeed in abolishing state aid to religion when a commutation bill was passed. Rights of the clergy were reserved and debentures of £100 000, payable in the colony, were bestowed on the Church of England (£58 000), Church of Rome (£23 000), Church of Scotland (£8000), Wesleyans (£7000), Free Church of Scotland (£3000) and Jews (£420).

Meanwhile a commission reported on a main line of railway and estimated the cost would be £750 000. To complete a survey and estimate, £6000 was voted by parliament but, as the northerners angrily pointed out, the public and not the local people (as in the case of the Deloraine line) had footed the bill for the survey, and this was inconsistent. Worse was to come because in April 1869 it appeared that the Launceston and Deloraine Company required £50 000 more than the earlier estimate to complete the line. This blow to the north did not however deter the government from authorizing the construction of a main line from Hobart Town to Launceston by a British firm for a total cost of £300 000. Captain Audley Coote represented the company and worked out the financial arrangements, after which a railway bill passed through parliament.

As that happened, the Western Line was officially opened for traffic in February 1870 when His Royal Highness, Alfred, Duke of Edinburgh turned the first sod. The railway age had come to Tasmania.

So also had another indication of the triumph of the colonists, for they now perceived, they thought, the final decline of the Aboriginal people.

Late in 1831, the remnants of the original inhabitants of the island were finally removed to Flinders Island from interim settlements at Swan Island and Guncarriage Island. Here the Aborigines were victims of government indifference and confusion of aims. As well, the ravages of pulmonary diseases reduced their numbers so much that by 1837 there were probably not enough left to recover and establish a viable population on their own.

In October 1847, some fourteen men, twenty-two women, five boys and five girls were transferred to the buildings of an old convict probation station at Oyster Cove, south of Hobart. Here they sunk into drunkenness and immorality, largely out of sight and out of mind and left without proper medical attention. The last man, William Lanne, died in 1869. His head was removed by Dr Lodewyk Crowther of the Colonial Hospital. A public uproar followed this mutilation in the interests of science, and the whereabouts of the head has never been traced with certainty.

Then on 8 May 1876 the last of the full-blood Aborigines in Tasmania also died, when Trugannini succumbed to bronchitis and asthma. Two years after her burial at the Cascades, the Royal Society took possession of the skeleton but for a century no thorough scientific examination of the remains was made. Ultimately as a result of pressure from people descended from the Aborigines, Trugannini's remains were ritually cremated and her ashes scattered in 1976.

In the opinion of N. J. B. Plomley, the foremost student of the Aborigines, the Aboriginal people failed to survive as a pure-blood group, so to speak, because in the first place they were particularly susceptible to introduced European diseases which could scarcely be cured or even alleviated by the medical procedures of the time. Secondly, there was no realization that the culture of these people had to be replaced by one which was meaningful to them. Especially useless was the inculcation of forms of Christianity by rote because it failed to come to terms with the spiritual beliefs of the Aborigines. Such crucial elements as the use of ochre for decoration and cultural coherence, the corroborees and language were taken from the Aborigines and their dignity fatally undermined. Thirdly, there no understanding that the Aborigines needed to be independent and conduct their own lives. Thus were they destroyed both in person and in terms of their culture—or so the Europeans thought.

3

Consolidation

In the twenty years from 1870 to 1890, the colony of Tasmania enjoyed a revival of fortune. Great changes were made in matters of public and private health, by the settlement of land in the north-west and north-east, and by public works. Railways continued to be laid down and mineral wealth was discovered and exploited. Tasmania shared in the increased investment made in the Australian colonies generally and there emerged a form of more coherent, purposeful and active government than had hitherto been the case. Yet the political history of this period as well as earlier and later was frequently centred upon the decisions of the all-powerful elitist Legislative Council which could and frequently did dictate to the people's House and to the population of the colony what laws or arrangements were to be permitted. An essential element of democratic government is risk and readiness to take a chance, underwritten by the opinion of the ordinary person. To this extent, the timidity and indeed reactionary character of the Legislative Council could not fail but be fatally damaging to the fabric of Tasmanian society, and its conduct in rejecting and hampering progressive work became so common as to be thought not remarkable.

In 1871 the Launceston and Western Railway was opened to the accompaniment of much display and self-congratulation in the north, but unhappily the times were bad, largely owing to the continued economic depression. It was said that costs of construction had been lavish and that hence the ability of the line to pay its way was reduced . . . and not the least of its difficulties was perceived to be the jealousy and spite of southern interests, exemplified in promoting a main line of railway between north and south and throwing obstacles in the way of the earnest and enterprising northerners.

The action of the government in spending public money to promote surveys of a main line infuriated Launceston and environs where residents repeatedly drew attention to the lack of government help they had received and the consequent large part played by expenditure of private capital. It became apparent that the new line had not fulfilled its promise and, in part due to the depressed state of northern agricultural and pastoral interests, was scarcely paying working expenses, let alone making the interest due to the government on the cost of construction. In these circumstances, it appeared that the government would be obliged to levy a rate but at the same time, to the continued fury of the north, in August 1871 it had signed a contract for construction of a main line by an English company. By August 1872, the western line was closed, with the government proposing to take over the plant at the same cost per mile as it had contracted for the main line, where construction started by the end of 1872, with 2000 navvies at work, playing their part in a consumer-led recovery.

In 1873 there were indeed signs of a revival in the economy and the western line began to pick up. The government decided to collect the railway rate due, but there was much murmuring at the government's overall proposal to clear the debt, thought by one party to be too generous and by the other not generous enough. But a rate was to be collected, insisted the government, and passive resistance was predicted. There was indeed resistance but it was most active, because when distrained goods were to be put up for sale to help meet the railway district's debts, rioting occurred, commencing at Launceston on 4 February 1874.

An effigy was burnt and dragged about the town and on the following day a large crowd gathered threateningly in front of the Commissariat Store where the seized articles were to be offered for sale. That night the crowd took over and the police panicked, leaving their superintendent alone. He was attacked and injured but finally the police rallied and dispersed the crowd. Next day attempts to swear in members of the fire brigade as special constables failed though young gentlemen volunteered. Some 2000 people by now had taken over Launceston and only reluctantly dispersed when the mayor, aldermen and police moved among them exhorting peace.

With this demonstration the agitation subsided, and the greater proportion of the moiety due for 1873 was collected, though the government shrunk from collecting the full amount owing. Much bitterness between north and south now existed and in June 1876 another railway difficulty appeared likely to arise when the first instalment of interest on the main line's £650 000 fell due. A controversy arose between the company and the ministry over

James ('Philosopher') Smith (1827–97), discoverer of Mt Bischoff tin mines whether or not the line had been completed as contracted. In 1886 there was a threat by the English directors in London to obstruct a £1 million loan sought by Tasmania unless the colony made concessions in respect of matters in dispute. This splendid example of imperial idealism was not publicized by the government and, when discovered, led to a vote of no confidence. This was properly muted, and failed.

A new railway to Scottsdale was opened in 1889 and by then the colony boasted 400 miles of permanent way. There had been none in 1870. The coming of railways to Tasmania was encouraged not only by enterprising northern interests but increasingly by mineral discoveries. Nothing of any importance in this department came to light, however, until in 1871 James 'Philosopher' Smith discovered tin at a place which came to be named Waratah, at Mt Bischoff, inland from the tiny settlement at Emu Bay on the north-west coast. In 1873 a company was formed at Launceston, to exploit what turned out to be the richest tin mine in the world. By 1880 it was producing 4000 tons a year worth some £350 000.

As well, some 2000 ounces of gold were recovered in 1870 and ten years later this figure had risen to 51 000 ounces, worth more than £200 000. Gold was located at Waterhouse in the north-east where the Great Tasmanian mine was promptly salted, although confidence was soon restored when it became clear that real gold was present. The principal quartz reefs there and at Fingal were said to have got into the hands of men whose Victorian experience had made them adept in the art of setting up bubble companies, so that local people were duped by Ballarat speculators.

In addition, deposits of silver were found east of the Penguin Creek on the north-west but did not prove the bonanza desired. In 1872 the Reedy Marsh and Black Boy mines in the Fingal district had generated a township of 650 people. In 1877, the best gold mine in Tasmania was discovered and alluvial and quartz mining produced some 30 000 ounces of gold in two years. In 1882 the New Golden Gate at Mathinna also began producing gold and the Tasmanian Iron Company exploited large deposits of iron ore, in the district of Leonardsburgh, near Beaconsfield, so named in 1879. The presence of chrome caused difficulties in 1877 in the production of iron and the enterprise never succeeded to any extent.

Most optimism, however, was centred upon the Mt Bischoff workings and by 1878 the town of Waratah was a sizeable one with cottages and slab huts, but situated in a very rugged country with high rainfall. Communication with the coast was most difficult and ore was originally removed by pack-horse and sent away for treatment on ships which came into the Penguin and Leith.

In all these encouraging circumstances, numbers of people coming to Tasmania, temporarily and permanently, increased sharply and had trebled from a low point in the 1860s to 10 000 a year by the end of the 1870s. Though emigration continued at a high figure as well, the total population of the colony increased by 14 per cent in the decade of the 1870s with a healthy diminution in the masculinity ratio, so that by 1880 there were 90 females for every 100 males, compared with the amazing figure of 46 in the early 1840s when convict transportation was at its height. In 1876, immigration exceeded emigration for the first time in years and the overall population increased from 101 000 to 115 000 in the decade of the 1870s, and then to 145 000 in the period to 1890. A substantial part of the increase in population was due to natural increase as the age structure and sex structure of the colonial population shifted to include a higher proportion of persons of marriageable age.

As Mt Bischoff continued to flourish, further attention was paid to the wild and tangled country to the west and south-west of that area. Mt Heemskirk was said to be rich in tin deposits and claims were taken up there and elsewhere in early 1878. New diggings appeared on the west coast in 1879 and although most were worked by Victorians who sent their earnings home, mineral wealth alleviated a threatened depression that year: £200 000 of gold was exported in 1880 out of total metal export of £362 000. By 1881, Waratah had so advanced that it supported a newspaper, and the government imported G. Thureau, a Victorian mining engineer, and appointed him geologist to examine the Heemskirk and Pieman River areas, which considerably impressed that gentleman with their potential. Inspired by visions of wealth and prosperity, the government subsidized a small steamer to run from Hobart to Macquarie Harbour and the Pieman, provided for construction of jetties and conducted surveys to lay a tram track from Trial Harbour to the Mt Heemskirk mines. That was in

1881, after even the Legislative Council approved some money for public works though it quickly got a hold of itself and reduced by half a vote to help the cutting of tracks in the wilds of western Tasmania.

Exploration was conducted between the Huon and Macquarie Harbour and the export of gold and tin continued to increase gratifyingly as Mt Heemskirk was further prospected by more than 300 mining companies formed by early 1882, compared to 90 in March the previous year. In 1883, Mt Bischoff paid its fifty-eighth dividend, worth a total of £6000, and in July 1885 the Van Diemen's Land Company, formed in 1825 for wool production but never successful, opened a railway from Emu Bay to Mt Bischoff in an effort to capitalize on freighting the valuable tin ore out of Waratah, the mine having paid nearly £600 000 in dividends to 1885.

The period from 1870 to around 1880 was marked by considerable advances in other areas of primary production. Exports rose in value from about £650 000 in 1870 to £1 500 000 in 1890, and though the number of sheep remained stable at about one and a half million, the production of wool increased from 4.2 million pounds to 9 million pounds. This was largely due to the vigorous work of James Whyte in supervising the removal of fluke from Tasmanian flocks by masterminding a dipping programme in the period 1869–80, at which time Tasmania was declared clean. Total government revenue went up during the twenty years from £270 000 to nearly £760 000. Acres in cultivation increased from 330 000 to 517 000 but acres in crop remained at 157 000 acres.

On the other hand, as acreage in some areas decreased, so it increased in the north-west and in the Huon. There had been a rise in apple production from 120 000 bushels to 155 000 in the period 1860–80, and this figure was more than doubled in the decade to the 1880s to 370 000 bushels, compensating for a decline in the timber trade. In the north-west, tons of potatoes produced went from 36 000 in 1870 to 73 000 in 1890. The number of trades and manufactories in the colony advanced slightly from 3200 to 3600 during the same period.

Under a section of the Land Settlement Act of 1870, selection was permitted and during the 1880s a total of nearly 5000 lots was sold, of which 20 per cent were in the county of Devon, on the north-west coast. The main features of this legislation were first, free selection at £1 an acre with one-third added by way of premium for credit; second, deferred payments extending over a period of fourteen years; third, disposal of half the purchase money upon construction of roads and bridges. The object was to encourage an industrious class without capital to make homes on heavily-timbered agricultural land. There was a right to select a maximum of 320 acres and provide for residence thereon until the land was paid for.

Between 1882 and 1885, in the north-west, 53 000 acres of Crown land was taken up, two steamers began trading to Melbourne, and there was an export trade of £75 000 in 1885, of which £37 000 was in potatoes and £15 000 in timber. Similarly land was being opened in the north-east, especially west of Scottsdale in the early 1880s, but two serious pests had appeared—rabbits spread all over the colony and the codlin moth wreaked havoc on the burgeoning apple industry.

Despite the encouraging signs, political conflict continued when diminished receipts in the early 1870s propelled the various governments of Tasmania towards again proposing direct taxes because of falling receipts from land sales and proposed relief to the railways. When in 1872 J. M. Wilson's government was obliged to foreshadow the imposition of a property and income tax of $2\frac{1}{2}$ per cent (5 per cent on absentees), the government fell and F. M. Innes succeeded to the premiership. He was granted six months' Supply on the understanding that he would not impose a direct tax. The result of this was a deficiency by mid-1873 of more than £100 000 in the budget, which Innes proposed to meet partly by a renewal of debentures and partly by alteration of the customs tariff, together with (he hoped) increased consumption of goods. He also proposed to relieve general revenue and land funds by throwing on local government areas certain charges for education, roads and bridges. This was judged inadequate and Innes' government was in turn voted out and succeeded by that of Alfred Kennerley in August 1873.

The treasurer in this administration was the merchant P. O. Fysh and in September he too proposed an income tax of 6d. in the pound ($2\frac{1}{2}$ per cent). But sure enough, the Legislative Council rejected the tax bill, with a view to defeat the government. The Council members did not have a very high standard of education.

Perhaps they also saw virtue in delay because the economy did indeed appear to be recovering so that perhaps the dreaded income tax would not be necessary after all. Perhaps something would turn up. And so it proved: when parliament next met, direct taxation was not spoken of by the government. Indeed, Kennerley's administration now proposed a very large outlay on public works in the remote districts. Would such a measure meet with the approval of the Council? No. That body threw out the government's measures, and parliament stood prorogued. For the second year running the Council rejected the principal ministerial measures.

The Council continued on its typical course: it rejected a public works bill because the legislation was unaccompanied by property tax proposals, which if they had been put forward would have only increased the Council's opposition.

In March 1878 W. R. Giblin, a new premier, began by taking unprecedented action against the Council. When it passed a bill to re-enact a proviso that the main line of railway could only be purchased by consent of parliament, Giblin thought so little of it that he induced all members of the House to combine and lay the measure aside without a division. But presently Giblin too was defeated in the House when by-elections told against him, and W. L. Crowther formed a government. He also at once fell foul of the Legislative Council which, in a chamber where only seven men were present, declined to consider the estimates and in December aggressively adjourned itself, after altering a money bill, for months. It then took action so that public servants went without salaries for nine weeks in mid-1879 until an uneasy agreement was concluded between the Houses, the Council persisting in its obstructive tactics till it was satisfied that ways and means were provided to bring income up to expenditure. Naturally enough, the Council rejected another income and property tax bill.

In these circumstances, yet another government was destroyed when Giblin's vote of no confidence led to the defeat of Crowther who then sought a dissolution and an election . . . but the governor denied him this and Giblin was enabled to form a fresh government in October 1879. He at once proposed to revise the tariff and remove anomalies, place a duty on ale and beer, a tax on real property of 9d. in the pound (3¾ per cent), and tax income from dividends, annuities and rents. He further proposed to raise £400 000 in England.

The governor's refusal to give Crowther an election was wise, although the Council remained as baleful as ever: in March 1880 it decided, in a move that was practically unconstitutional, to adjourn for three months in opposition to the wishes of the government. By this a debenture bill for £450 000 (reduced by £200 000 by the Council) was lost in the consequent prorogation, the Council having earlier rejected public works proposals.

At the same time, Christopher O'Reilly, the new Minister for Lands and Works (a department created by Wilson in 1869) brought forward an important public works scheme involving £163 000. There now appeared to have been an erosion of opposition in both houses, with Crowther and Thomas Reibey, member for Westbury and premier 1876–7, having been rejected by their erstwhile followers. A good deal of the credit for continued stability in government must go to Giblin, his political skills undoubtedly aided greatly by increasing prosperity and the work of one Samuel Henry in effecting a sort of coalition. But the Council still showed fight—it rejected £72 000 for public works and refused to vote a salary to Henry, who had been appointed to an office under the Land Tax Act. Chapman and Crowther led this opposition in the Council, displaying as it was factionalism of the worst kind.

When parliament met in August 1883, the government renewed its plans to reduce by half the duties on tea and sugar and abolish the duty on machinery. As well, a public works scheme totalling an expenditure of nearly £1 million was also proposed. When the Legislative Council met to consider this most pressing matter, insofar as its abilities would permit, it could not muster a quorum, but finally rejected a bill for destruction of the codlin moth, considerably amended a measure which sought to destroy rabbits, and agreed to consider the proposed huge public works (including railways) proposals that day six months. This led to public outrage and northern members of the Council received such a very hostile reception when they journeyed home that shortly thereafter the bill was agreed to.

But the Council soon rallied after this setback and splendidly demonstrated its perception of high purpose and sensitivity to colonial welfare by rejecting a bill to prohibit the practice of shooting live pigeons from traps, and introducing business which involved money and which was therefore carefully calculated to annoy the House of Assembly.

Then Giblin resigned because of bad health and, on his suggestion, was succeeded by Adye Douglas, with a similar ministry. As a legacy of his widely-admired administration, however, Giblin left a successful proposal to give the vote for the lower House to all ratepayers, instead of only those rated at £7 a year and above, and to allow wage-earners who made £80 or more a year similarly to vote. By 1894, numbers enabled to vote for the lower House had doubled, as had those permitted to vote for the Council.

The colonists of Tasmania, like their fellow Britons elsewhere in the Australias, as the colonies were sometimes termed, and New Zealand, always attached very great importance to their links with the Old Country, or Home. Especially was this so among the literate, although the inarticulate majority also cheered the Crown in tune with their more consciously loyal elders and betters. The height of imperial loyalty was manifested on the occasion of royal visits such as that by Prince Alfred, 1869–70. In 1887 it was the Queen's gold jubilee and in June this was marked by wide-ranging demonstrations and manifestations of patriotism, by a race meeting in the afternoon at Hobart and a general illumination in the evening. The governor reported with quiet pride on the enthusiastic and orderly bearing of the large crowd when he walked incognito through it. On 22 June there was a review of the defence forces and a huge procession marched to the scene. Addresses were handed to the Crown's representative and he in turn read out a telegram from the Secretary of State for the Colonies, sending Her Majesty's cordial thanks to the women and girls of Tasmania for their loyal address. Schoolchildren marched through a tent in their thousands and each was presented with a commemorative medal and jubilee cakes. Fireworks were displayed at night and there was a grand ball on the evening of the 23rd at Government House, to which more than 900 distinguished guests were invited. Unfortunately it was a very wet night in Hobart and only 550 attended, but it was impossible to overstate the intense loyalty of the people to the person and throne of Queen Victoria and tribute was paid to the excellent work of the Mayor of Hobart, Mr C.

Harbottle, as chairman of the United Jubilee Committee. To mark the festivities, some forty persons sentenced to gaol for minor offences were freed in honour of the occasion. No counter-demonstrations were reported.

Imperialism as it had emerged in Tasmania was very closely linked to military and naval exhibitions of British power. A Flying Squadron anchored in the Derwent in 1870, during the visit of Prince Alfred, and the conduct of its sailors was recorded as admirable, only three of their number deserting. On the other hand, such visits were not always marked by manifestations of harmony and light for the Empire: H.M.S. *Wolverene* was obliged to complain about the particularly virulent form of syphilis contracted by its loyal crew in Hobart Town in 1877. It was with much shame that the local authorities were led to establish a contagious diseases hospital for the incarceration and cure of females apprehended or who admitted themselves for treatment.

Certain of the Tasmanians were also upset when it was decided to bring away all troops from the Australian colonies in 1870, a departure perceived by some with limitless imagination as equivalent to the withdrawal of the Roman legions from Britain. The severing of even such a slight but tangible link with Home exposed faraway Tasmania even more to the cold winds of isolation and hence reinforced the urgency of loyalty to the Mother Country, the Crown and the Protestant succession: in the Franco-Prussian war the Protestants of Tasmania tended to support Prussia and the Catholics to take the part of France. Similarly when the Duke of Genoa visited and appeared at the Government House levee on the occasion of the Queen's birthday in 1873, the Duke and his brother officers were received with much cordiality but the Catholic clergy as a body kept aloof.

There was a history of tension between Catholics and Protestants in Tasmania; it had been manifested during meetings supporting the Crimean War when Catholic spokesmen were obliged to insist that they were no less loyal to Britain than were the Protestants. Then in 1879 a most interesting example of sectarianism emerged with the visit to Hobart Town of the apostate Catholic Pastor Charles Chiniquy. Such were the passions aroused that the Volunteers were called out in aid of the civil power, a question arose of whether the city council was justified, let alone wise, to let the Town Hall for a meeting which was a

The connection with Home

sure recipe for religious strife; and much energy was spent on discussing the timing of an appeal from the Catholic bishop to restrain the Catholic element from violence.

Chiniquy had a lurid line in ribald slanders of Catholic women and, although he was clearly unhinged, this did not preclude support from persons who should have known better.

The education of young colonists left a good deal to be desired in the first fifty or sixty years of the settlement of the colony, and it was not till 1869 that the first general examination of teachers was conducted by the Board of Education. Few teachers were systematically trained. Possession of literary talent was thought enough to lead to promotion but the Board now said no to this. As for the schools, many buildings were found to be utterly inadequate and some few even lay in ruin, many children were aged more than ten before they came to school, and then were removed for field labour. Because their attendance was fitful and irregular, many forgot what they had learnt and were a handicap to the children who attended regularly. Indeed, absenteeism was frequently judged as immeaurably worse than no attendance at all, but local school boards appointed under the Education Act of 1869 were understandably most reluctant to use their influence with neighbours in urging regular school attendance.

In short, there was inadequate provision for training teachers, absence of serious local responsibility, the want of power to enforce conditions, and a shortage of funds and inducements to make the absolutely necessary improvements. Perhaps most importantly of all, the teachers were paid pitifully small salaries largely because local school fees went unpaid in far too many cases. In seeking to collect weekly fees, the teacher met with the most miserable shifts and excuses to avoid payment, and especially was he or she financially insecure in the many small schools.

School inspection was minimal because there were so few officials of the Board, and in 1875 one such felt it necessary to put in a plea for the assistance of men with an aptitude for bush travelling, unlimited capacity for roughing it and an ability to swim unfordable rivers in the north of the colony. The reading books of the popular Irish National Schools System were also to be criticized; especially when they really required to be translated into colonial English when such a passage as this appeared to confront little Tasmanians: 'The pearl consists of concentric coats of the same substance as that which forms the mother-of-pearl of the shell; they are produced by the extravasation of a lapidifying fluid, secreted in the organs of the animals, and filtered by its glands.'

In 1885 a new Education Act sought to correct some of these many deficiencies and there followed a year later the establishment of the first technical school in Hobart, followed by another one in Launceston in 1888.

Some of the inhabitants of the colony were not concerned with education of their children but all were concerned with their health

Late nineteenth-century guide for tourists

and its precarious state. The conditions of urban and rural living came under close scrutiny in the 1880s and a series of reports on the cities of Launceston and Hobart, followed by others on rural centres, revealed the supposed causes of those diseases which struck down colonists. Smallpox was a particular scourge and such colonists as Dr E. S. Hall, an energetic physician and social reformer, never lost an opportunity to drop a few improving words about vaccination and its benefits. The poverty-stricken among the Tasmanians, however, regarded the treatment with great wariness, suspecting that it might bring on the disease, or transmit or originate others, especially those of a loathsome character. Only outbreaks of smallpox would lead parents to have their children vaccinated.

Typhoid fever was a killer and following deaths from that disease in the mid-1870s, a report was required by the government on the sanitary arrangements in the capital of the colony. It emerged that reliable data were non-existent but that typhoid, diphtheria and other such diseases were understood most frequently to arise from the people breathing gases which emanated from sewage and decomposing animal and vegetable matter, from consumption of impure drinking water, and from over-crowding and want of ventilation in dwellings. Other diseases such as scarlatina were rendered more virulent and propagated with greater rapidity by the same causes.

Similar conditions existed in Launceston, where deaths had increased in the early 1870s although the number of inhabitants had not, and similarly the chief medical officer blamed inadequate drainage and sewerage, with the contents of patent water-closets reported to flow into open gutters and with no complete and enforced use of earth-closets.

Pig-sties abounded in settled areas of Tasmania, offensive to sight and injurious to public health, and abattoirs exhibited horrible scenes of offal disposal. In Hobart the south side of the Cascade Road was a ditch of sewage filth, putrefying and poisoning the air, but the greatest nuisance and dangers were thought to be the privy cesspits where human excrement was often kept for years without removal, saturating the adjacent soil and polluting the air with pestilential emanations, so that earth-closets at least were required.

By the end of the 1870s, the whole question of public health required attention, not least the matter of the Hobart Town Rivulet, which was an abominable open sewer into which faecal matter was discharged together with soap suds and other putrefactive elements.

No one knew why diseases which had been virtually unknown in earlier years had quite suddenly made their appearance in the colony and Dr Hall remained untiring in drawing attention to their dangers and origins, as he perceived them. Smallpox prevention was under way elsewhere, he thundered, such as in Worcester, Massachusetts, and action was taken in 1883 when by a Public Health Act for Hobart it was laid down that new cesspits were to be constructed, defective ones removed and all to be filled in by the end of 1886. In addition, an overall drainage plan for Hobart was signalled and the pail method of collecting nightsoil pronounced a great step forward in the fight against disease. Throughout the colony a Public Health Act came into force on 1 January 1885. It led to the establishment of local boards of health which closed down cesspits and, it was reported, banished typhoid from areas where it had hitherto prevailed every autumn.

In the mid-1880s, Alfred Mault, engineering inspector of the board of health, described the situation in Hobart as still deplorable. Sewerage arrangements were generally chaotic and no plan of them appeared to exist, cesspits were very imperfectly constructed and emptied at uncertain intervals, the gutters of the city were swept at varying intervals by Corporation scavengers, sewage lodged in every hollow, and faecal matter was carted to farms at New Town and Sandy Bay and used as manure without being disinfected.

By 1885, in Launceston there were 130 houses connected with the sewers, 70 water-closets substituted for cesspits, 250 premises cleaned and 92 disinfected, 86 notices served for defective privy construction, 186 for defective drainage, 250 for filthy houses, and 25 for filthy stables, cowsheds and piggeries; the yearly visitations of typhoid and diphtheria still occurred. Especially singled out for attention was a ten-acre block on the Inveresk Swamp which supported a population of 469 souls, about four times the average density of population in Launceston. Two-thirds of the cases of fever were traced to the swamps between the railway and the North Esk River, and twenty of these came from a block at the corner of the Esplanade and Invermay Road. One of the problems in Launceston was that a plan of sewerage for the town had been adopted in the 1850s with the result that sewage was discharged straight into the Tamar River.

As if that was not bad enough, it was reported in 1886 that cemeteries with one exception were not suitably placed, so that the Scotch cemetery in High Street drained down the steep hill where a rivulet formed in rainy weather mingled its waters with those of the overflow from the Lord Street reservoirs, so forming part of the supply to houses in Hampton Vale.

In the best lodging houses in the town were to be found four rooms in which were seventeen beds, and the premises were actually licensed to contain no fewer than thirty-two. One room had four beds jammed into it and a tenement in Bathurst Street had sixteen rooms let out in lodgings of one, two and three rooms which were occupied by twenty people, living in filthy conditions.

Similar conditions existed in Hobart where in the Glebe Town a four-room cottage was occupied by eight persons, of whom four were adults.

Rural slums were also known: at Brighton a man named Shearman and his wife and seven children, dressed in sacking, occupied one room only, and at Avoca the local policeman's family had the noisome cells between their rooms. It was no wonder that smallpox continued.

In the late 1870s, 'fever' was also notified at the Furneaux Islands. First settled in the late eighteenth century, these islands came to be the home of descendants of Tasmanian Aborigines, sealers and some ex-convicts. By the mid-nineteenth century, there was an established community on Guncarriage, Woody, Tin Kettle, Cape Barren and Clarke Islands. Mutton birds provided subsistence and a valuable export. Dr E. P. Vines, of Formby on Mersey (Devonport), visited to check the 'fever' and did what he could to encourage cleanliness and fumigation of the houses, in the course of his duties offering interesting comment on the culture of these descendants of the original people of Van Diemen's Land.

Tasmania's origins haunted the island and promotion of the colony as a 'sanatorium of the south' was calculated to distance the society as far as possible from the horrors and shame of transportation and the destruction of the Aboriginal people. After a lengthy and irritable debate with the imperial authority, the surviving Port Arthur prisoners were transferred to Hobart. A financial arrangement was concluded by which it was possible for the British government to foot the bill for transportation as late as the 1930s, in the hypothetical case of a youthful convict transported in the early 1850s reappearing to claim maintenance in his or her nineties. So close did the convict era approach Tasmania, and indeed from time to time old convicts came under notice right through the century. As late as 1882 the grim imprint of the transportation system appeared when an ex-prisoner of 1852 figured in a murder. It was a pathetic case. The man, employed as a groom and milkman at Campbell Town and dwelling in a kitchen, killed a police constable when a conflict arose over the ex-convict's desire to have a turkey to keep with his pet parrot.

Right to the end of the century, persons in gaol still included those listed as 'free by servitude' and there were many institutions which owed at least some of their objects of charity and cost to the transportation system. In 1870 there were no fewer than 700 absolutely destitute children in Launceston and two Ragged Schools, one at the wharf and the other in Brisbane Street. In most cases relief was given in the form of provisions but when a standard uniform was issued to the deserving, it provoked a significant cry of 'Tench! Tench!', the convict slang for penitentiary.

But the revival of the economy and a return towards demographic normality generated a spirit of optimism and energy. This was apparent in all areas of Tasmanian public life. In the early 1870s the Tasmanian Public Library was created by act of parliament, with Alfred Kennerley chairman of trustees, and in 1886 another act brought into existence the Tasmanian Museum and Botanical Gardens; there was a huge amount of public interest in the introduction of salmon for sport and commerce; government moved in to decrease the hours at which public houses might be open and to control their general conduct; the administration of Tasmania contributed on a pound-for-pound basis to the various road trusts which were struggling to provide transport of the utmost importance in the newly-settled areas where bad roads were sometimes positively dangerous; an act of 1873 made provision for retreats or houses for treatment of habitual inebriates, and appointed commmissions to enquire into prison discipline and lunatic asylums; moves were made which led to the establishment of the university; a government analyst's office was founded so that imported and other goods might be tested scientifically before issue to the public; an inspector of mines was appointed in 1882; a Hobart Tramway Company bill was drafted in 1884 and in 1885 government sought to control the conditions and hours of work of women and children against strong opposition from such as jam manufacturers and proprietors of woollen mills who considered that ten hours a day for such persons was perfectly reasonable.

An act of 1885 laid down that no women could be employed for more than ten hours a day, or children for eight, except for saleswomen in shops where goods were exposed for sale on Saturday evening, or children employed in jam factories from January to March and in October who could be employed for nine hours. In addition, the eight-hour day came to prevail by consent and custom (though it never got through parliament) except for agricultural labourers and adult males employed in shops.

Reform and progressive legislation characterized the period. Some colonists strove to raise the age of female consent from twelve years to sixteen and generally reform the law as it related to females; an enquiry recommended that the various friendly

Public transport in Hobart driven by hydro-electricity

societies be controlled so that liabilities for medical and monetary relief in sickness and death could be met; the centralization of the municipal and territorial police was recommended by a parliamentary committee after evidence of local favouritism and territorial men as ragged in appearance as Falstaff's recruits. In 1885 a conservator of forests was appointed under the State Forests Act and a beginning made on saw-mill reservations and state reserves in the very important timber industry. Hospitals were opened at Waratah and Latrobe; the government appointed an inspector of fisheries, the Tasmanian Government Railways was formed and in the late 1880s the eminent engineer C. Napier Bell began issuing a series of reports on harbour works to be conducted at such crucial places as Macquarie Harbour.

But a great depression was casting its shadows over all the colonies and though the mining industry was booming, on 3 August 1891 there was a catastrophe—the Bank of Van Diemen's Land failed.

There had earlier been indications of difficulties or change of direction in the money market, though they were masked in the case of Tasmania as elsewhere in the Australian colonies by the boom of the 1880s which, in turn, led to the impression that the sky was the limit in terms of investment, profit and development of the colony. Yet prices generally had been dropping in Europe and North America, a phenomenon related to cheaper methods of production and a contraction in the supply of money.

The collapse of investments made by the prominent London house of Barings bank in its South American economic colonies signalled an end to Australian prosperity in the late nineteenth century. Those who sought to investigate the causes of this and the associated depression found allies and opponents no matter what forms of analysis they used and what conclusions they drew. Baffled observers could fall back only on a stock response commonly and with a touch of desperation termed 'a loss of confidence'. When British supplies of capital were withdrawn from the Australian colonies or sharply reduced, there was a chain reaction. Cautious or timid, wise or unscrupulous, certain speculators removed themselves from the market and put their paper investments and share scrip into hard cash. Lesser men followed suit, rumours of impending collapses gathered strength and those who had looked up to respectable colonists and institutions for

The Bank of Van Diemen's Land raffled, 1894

guidance and a nod of approval discovered that their examplars, especially in Melbourne, had been rash or foolish at best and rogues at worst.

The collapse of the Bank of Van Diemen's Land was the first serious bank failure in a miserable decade for Australia as a whole. Not only was the 1890s characterized by the spectacular failure of financial institutions but as well a prolonged drought racked the principal eastern colonies and strikes of unparalled intensity convulsed them. The common liberal belief that labour and capital had the same interests fell to pieces as class conflict emerged when first the shipping industry and then the pastoral and mining interests were the scene of bitter and protracted disputes.

Established for upwards of seventy years, the Bank of Van Diemen's Land had become a byword for steadiness and reliability in comparison with more rackety money-lenders and, indeed, enjoyed an impressive reputation for probity. Public trust was misplaced. The bank fell victim to greed associated with risky lending and business ventures, reinforced by the bold example offered by Victorian institutions.

When the bank was ultimately wound up by act of parliament, a Royal Commission had concluded that an alleged £30 000 due by other banks was in fact overdraft permission from the London and Westminster Bank, and that another £50 000 in coin and bullion put on the balance sheet as an asset existed only in the febrile imagination of the directors. The closure of such an institution came as a bombshell to the public, because no indication had been given to any of the branches of the bank that it was in difficulties.

Such was the impact of the crash that for many years afterwards Tasmanians dated events from 'the year the V.D.L. Bank went broke'.

4

Expansion

Manifestly the result of duplicity, the collapse of the Bank of Van Diemen's Land was felt particularly on the west coast mining fields in which it had a deep financial interest. Ultimately the assets of the bank were disposed of by a lottery conducted by George Adams, he whose sweepstakes had become immensely popular and been removed from both New South Wales and Queensland by legislation outlawing the enterprise. Impressed by the difficulties thrown in the way of a man without government influence, Adams came to Tasmania. The act of parliament necessary to legalize this novel method of winding up a bank was finally passed in 1893 and, animated with the same spirit, three years later another act helped solve the colony's financial difficulties by presenting Tattersalls with a license to conduct lotteries. The ostensible aim was to crack down on illegal gambling totes and usher in a government-controlled lottery. These decisions were accompanied by enormous public uproar.

The depression led the government to its traditional method of drastic retrenchment and although in 1896 the colonial debt was £8 million, revenue improved mainly due to the increase in output of gold, silver and coal and a steady production of tin. The plain man took other steps to make ends meet in hard times and there was an outbreak of arson for the insurance, an offence which the police found very difficult to detect though substantial rewards were offered when incendiarism was beyond doubt. In general, however, the mining industry held its own despite the financial crisis and a disastrous fall in the price of silver.

Unemployment alarmed parliament and people, and by 1893, with great strikes signalling the downfall of class co-operation, it was urged that public works be advanced, and this was done all over the colony. Yet casualties continued. In the case of the

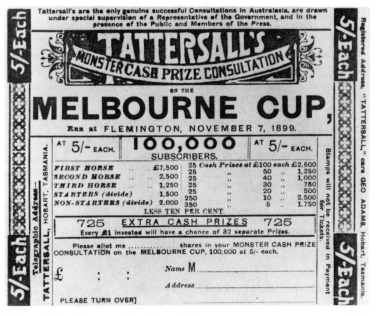

Tattersalls Melbourne Cup ticket, 1899

Hobart Benevolent Society, there was an increase in the number of families on the books from 130 in 1893 to 602 in 1894, and the Society was hard-pressed to supply enough relief in the form of soup, blankets and clothing, wood and coal, during the winter. In Launceston, the sister society had its heaviest years in 1893 and 1894, reporting many more cases of real poverty among the respectable class than were normally dealt with as a result of the secretary seeking them out because the families were too ashamed to make personal application for aid. During 1894, 2000 casual cases were relieved, and at the end of that year, there were 56 men, 116 women and 179 children on the Launceston society's permanent roll. In the May following there were 72 men, 142 women and 280 children, many in the unemployed class, with a total of 974 individuals assisted during the year. The society urged subscribers not to assist beggars because the money presented to them was promptly spent on drink, but to refer them to 239 Charles Street. It was also suspected that a large number of children were imposing on the decent people with spurious tales of want and misery.

The depression also caused trouble in the area of land settlement. Experience of the act of 1870 showed that the yearly payments on 320-acre blocks were too much and the residential clauses were not enforced. Following the relative failure of this legislation to secure bona fide settlement, it was repealed by another act of 1890. This rendered it compulsory for selectors 'habitually' to reside on their allotment until the purchase money was paid, and to effect substantial improvements thereon. In 1893, however, it was discovered that 130 000 acres were unproductive and seriously in arrears. Selectors were then asked to comply with the conditions of purchase, but with little result because the depression made it impossible for the government to act without causing hardship. Thus another act was passed which authorized the government to postpone payment of instalments for up to five years on payment of a 5 per cent interest, or an offer of the alternative proposal of transferring instalments paid on the whole to purchase any portion not less than half the area of the block.

This was accounted successful generally, but by the mid-1890s it was claimed that the largest proportion of the best agricultural land remained locked up in sheep and cattle runs, and the question

Hauling piles to the shipping place, Adventure Bay, 1906

was raised of whether such lands should not be bought back by the government because these owners were driving the industrious settler away. Thus closer settlement schemes began. Surveys went forward, especially in the north-west where in such an area as Riana, south of the Penguin, applicants were mostly friends or related to each other, and formed a self-contained settlement where they very rapidly improved their holdings, usually less than 50 acres. Some of these settlers presumably came into the area on the basis of legislation providing for purchase during eighteen years at £1 an acre, with one-third added for credit, the maximum selection to be 50 acres, with the government providing costs of survey.

Another remote area further settled was King Island. From 1864 to 1887 this was held under lease and used as a bush run for stock. A surveyor was sent in 1887 and subsequently forty-one selections totalling 6000 acres were applied for and six pastoral leases issued. Settlers principally engaged in pastoral pursuits because stock fattened with marvellous rapidity on the native grasses; there was a fortnightly communication with the mainland during spring and summer. In 1896 about 100 people lived on the island, and 400 fat cattle had been shipped, chiefly to Launceston. Sheep were also run and low-lying land improved by ploughing and sowing red and white clover, the cattle having suffered when permitted to run free because they fed on poisonous tares. Dairy farming was projected, selections were fenced and houses, roads and a jetty under construction.

The importance for the colony of agriculture was marked by the formation of a Council of Agriculture in 1892. Councillors were drawn from all over the island, a government entymologist appointed, the services of a veterinary surgeon availed of, twenty-eight local boards established and a sturdy *Agricultural Journal* issued. Related to this development was the formation of dairy, butter and cheese co-operatives and factories at Table Cape, Burnie and Launceston with others foreshadowed, and a travelling dairy designed to show producers the latest methods. Producers responded to this initiative as a rule, it was reported, by sending their wives and daughters to be instructed, striking evidence of how labour in the industry was deployed.

At the same time, the fruit export business grew and from the 1890s experiments such as sending fruit in ventilated holds to the

English market began to succeed and methods of pruning trees in the shape of a wine-glass improved yields. But dispute arose over the method of control of shipments, with well-grounded fears that the unscrupulous and greedy growers and shippers would ruin a prospectively good market by consigning windfalls and other such fruit unfit for market.

Exports to London averaged around 150 000 bushels in the early 1890s, worth about £50 000, with acreages of orchard from 70 at Frankford to more than 1000 at Glenorchy. Hostile tariffs militated severely against the successful export of jams and fruit to other colonies though there was a market.

Timber-cutting was also an important industry in the south, although since first settlement of Van Diemen's Land, timber had been exploited wherever could be found such very valuable and unique species as the Huon pine, King William and pencil pine, as well as the common stringybark variety. Associated with the felling of trees for building materials, was their use as railway sleepers, paving blocks and furniture. A wattle-bark industry existed for tanning, and this began to create anxiety in the 1890s because there was only a lax method of licensing. In addition, such few forestry experts as were disinterested warned strongly against unrestricted hewing down of trees, especially the rare sort. Discussion and action on the forestry front continued to be distinguished by a conflict between those who put immediate gain foremost and those who counselled a comprehensive system of forest management, pioneered by G. S. Perrin in 1886.

Two pests particularly affected agriculturists—rabbits and the codlin moth, with thistles also. Many efforts were made to rid the colony of the former but it proved beyond effective control, largely because there was no effective wide-ranging poison: the pest flourished on both private and Crown land, recognizing no boundaries, and because the government land was frequently only thinly occupied it was almost impossible to police. In addition, the industry of selling rabbit skins became a vested interest and meant that the rabbit was not trapped much in the summer but left till winter when the pelt was of superior quality and worth more. So despite many warnings from those who predicted that the hangman would find work for youths and others who led wild lives trapping rabbits and other animals, the inroads of the creature on pasture and hence on agricultural production became and remained a substantial problem.

More success was ultimately to be achieved in checking the codlin moth but for a time it too appeared to endanger the entire fruit industry, not a little aided as it was when fruit boards refrained from invoking the full penalties, such as they were, against their own members.

At quite a different level, pleas were made by some colonists for the further destruction of the Tasmanian tiger and the native eaglehawk for their attacks on livestock, but in these cases the animals were scarce enough to be subject of final solutions by local people.

In both rural and urban areas, typhoid continued to be feared, for despite the acceptance of the germ theory of transmission of disease, medical science remained without the medication to check or cure such scourges. The Central Board of Health in Tasmania watched anxiously for signs of typhoid and other dreaded diseases and at the beginning of the last decade of the century rejoiced that deaths from typhoid had been only 49 in 1890 compared with 84 in 1880 and 113 in 1889. One practice which certain colonists had brought with them to Tasmania was thought to contribute to the spread of disease such as diphtheria. This was the custom kept up by Irish settlers of conducting wakes, especially prevalent in certain districts. His Grace the Catholic Archbishop of Hobart was informed of medical men's well-founded fears of the practice of exposing the corpse and a circular letter was then issued to all Catholic clergy requesting them to do their best to discourage such customs, advice from such a quarter thought to be effectual.

Concern for health was attested by thousands of advertisements in the papers for cure-alls. 'FREE—To all NERVOUS DISABILITY Sufferers, a certain, easy and permanent SELF CURE. Having cured myself after years of suffering, misery and loss of money to quack doctors, I will send full particulars FREE on receipt of an addressed envelope for reply. Address—A Miner, G.P.O. Sydney'. The magic potion supplied by 'A Miner' at £1 1s. an ounce turned out to be Peruvian Bark in powdered form, the ordinary retail price being 1s. an ounce.

By 1897 there had been passed an act containing most of the provisions desired by the Central Board of Health: infectious and contagious diseases were better defined and more complete provisions made for their notification; wilful exposure of the body of a person who had died of any infectious disease was made penal; the powers of local boards of health to prevent the spread of infectious disease and to control the milk supply in their districts was extended and the closing of polluted wells rendered easier. The Board regretted that the government had made no provision for sanitary inspection of dwellings before occupation, had not permitted the Board to approve local appointments, and made no provision for preventing streams being polluted by water-closets.

By 1896 the necessary mapping for the drainage of Hobart had been done and, a report on sewerage recommending discharge into the sea at Macquarie Point having been completed in 1892, the Board sought parliamentary approval to conduct the work, inserting into its request the information that 'fever' was most directly attributable to bad drainage.

But typhoid continued to lay low the population in certain areas and in 1897 there were more cases than ever before, though fewer deaths than in 1891. The disease was particularly rife in mining areas and among hop-pickers where it raged as usual among those who seasonally migrated to the hopfields. Local boards of health were urged to make special measures concerning proper housing for the hop-pickers and especially to prevent the fouling of streams which flowed through or by the hopgrounds.

Some blamed infectious diseases on the disposal of nightsoil by the disgusting pan system which merely transmitted germs. The Metropolitan Drainage Board in Hobart stated with all the emphasis at its command that typhoid would never be subdued except with a comprehensive drainage system; and produced figures from Munich and Sydney to show how appalling was the situation in Tasmania. As if to drive home the point, in 1898 the surgeon of H.M.S. *Wallaroo* communicated with Hobart to enquire whether it was safe to permit his men ashore. The Board that year gloomily noted the highest death-rate in Tasmania since 1892, there having been nearly 2400 cases of infectious disease noted, by far the highest ever.

The melancholy bills of mortality revealed 125 deaths from phthisis, 99 from cancer and 53 from flu; there were 802 cases of typhoid reported of which 83 were fatal, measles 912 (45), scarlatina 550 (7) and diphtheria 98 (10). The death rate from measles was the highest since 1881 and half the flu cases were recorded in the largely rural north-west quarter alone. In the new mining settlement at Queenstown there were 24 cases of typhoid in 1899, lending point to the opening of a hospital there. Health authorities concluded that the source of disease was on the Conglomerate Creek (known as The Piggeries) because polluted water was drunk by the reckless or indifferent class of people who dwelt there.

During this period of the 1890s, Hobart continued to decline and Launceston to increase in population and importance. This was in part due to land settlement in the north-west and north-east. During the last twenty years of the century, attention was drawn more and more to settlement in the north-west, where a strong Wesleyan element congregated, and to the Huon Valley, where a high proportion of Catholics took up residence.

Of greater short-term importance in the development of the north was the mineral boom, embodied in the tin-mining industry, especially at Mt Bischoff, mining of coal at Fingal, and gold. New northern railways continued to be opened, frequently against the better judgement of professional railwaymen who correctly perceived that many such lines would never pay their way and were only laid down in response to 'development' without long-range analyses. But these changes in the structure of the colony's economy and pattern of settlement were dwarfed by mineral discoveries of world importance in one of the most inhospitable parts of the island.

This was signalled, up to a point, by the institution of the office of Inspector of Mines. G. Thureau's first official report revealed the wealth so characteristic of the mining industry and the presence of the soulless pirates who always hung about it. For instance, eight men were killed in mines in 1882, including one man who perished in a tin mine, leaving a wife and seven children. They received the sum of £10 in compensation. At that time, some 1500 men were working on auriferous fields and 2500 on the tin fields.

Then in 1885 Thureau reported on something new: at a place called Mt Zeehan (named by Matthew Flinders in 1799 after one of Tasman's ships in 1642) silver-lead deposits had been located. The same year it became known that gold was discovered at the King River and at a place named Mt Lyell, in the same area of the west. Ironically a year later the conservator of forests reported having been at Mt Lyell and its environs after pushing through the bush from Waratah. In describing the pine forests along the Pieman River and especially those of the Gordon, he stressed that these age-old stands of timber must for ever be carefully guarded against devastation by man because under a proper system of forestry management they would yield money in perpetuity.

Then about 200 miners were drawn to a spot named Linda in such desolate country that strong men were reduced to wrecks reaching the area where some copper was found but chiefly gold. That was in 1886.

The most notable discovery was one made by James Crotty, an Irish-born prospector who bought an interest in an outcrop called the Iron Blow, found to be very rich in gold (and unbeknown, in copper). By mid-1889, some thirty tons of copper had been sent to New South Wales for treatment, but transport difficulties led to a lull in the working of the deposit.

At the same time further evidence of Tasmania's mineral wealth appeared with the discovery of a silver-bearing ore at Mt Dundas, seven miles north-east of Mt Zeehan, a field which excited very great attention and where some 16 000 acres were marked off for lease. By 1890 the new boom town of Zeehan housed a population of 2500 and the mining industry had never presented so hopeful a prospect. The great silver discoveries led to more prospecting and fresh finds; capital poured in for investment in the mines, proposals for railways and harbour works, not to mention bold gas and electricity enterprises, and a government railway line from Strahan to Zeehan opened in 1892.

For a while it appeared that the entire west coast of the colony of Tasmania was composed of precious metals. Incredulous and credulous investors were only partly checked by the crash of the Bank of Van Diemen's Land. Money was squandered, inadequate machinery employed and management conducted by incompetents. Confidence men swarmed on to the field or remained in the vicinity of the stock exchanges. Capital came from everywhere and immigrants from the stricken colony of Victoria, the economy of which lay in ruins after the dizzy splendours of the 1880s and the construction of Marvellous Melbourne had revealed the mixed blessing of land boomers.

In Mt Lyell and associated mines the colony had a source of dream-like wealth for those shrewd, able, diligent or unscrupulous

TASMANIAN
SMELTING COMPANY
LIMITED.

GENERAL VIEW
OF WORKS.

SCALE — 64 FEET TO AN INCH.

Smelting works at Zeehan, 1899

enough to tap it. Assays of copper, gold and silver led the American Dr Edward Peters, one of the world's most eminent metallurgists, to report that in the past twenty years he had not seen a mining and metallurgical proposition that promised so certainly to be a great and enduring property. Bowes Kelly, the manager of the Mt Lyell Mining and Railway Company, was about to make a fortune (Crotty had already made one and left most of it to finish St Patrick's Cathedral, Melbourne): the immense outcrop of hematite called the Iron Blow, worked for gold till 1890 after being traced up the Linda Valley, was found to have a large mass of pyrites standing in close connection and it was that which responded so richly to smelting for copper. This lode appeared to descend for ever into the earth, and therefore appeared limitless in practical terms; the ore was double the richness of that found at the fabled Rio Tinto mine in Spain.

For the year ending 1 July 1894, the value of mineral output in Tasmania was the highest in its history at a total of £707 000, with nearly 3500 people working in the mining industry. A survey of twenty-one miles of railway from Strahan to the mines commenced. By 1895 the Mt Lyell railway, from Teepookana to Queenstown, was approaching completion with rails laid and passengers and freight already being carried, and there was a light steam tramway from Zeehan going some sixteen miles into the Mt Reid country. At Zeehan, a School of Mines had been established by the miners themselves, and had forty-nine students with voluntary lecturers offering the earnest mining student such subjects as mineralogy, chemistry, assaying, mathematics, mine surveying and mechanical drawing. A mining culture was suddenly established in a wilderness which had known only the nomadic Aborigines for 12 000 years. El Dorado appeared in the most inhospitable part of the colony, and investors invested parliament with schemes to supply electric power and railways, and to be cut in on the apparent fortunes awaiting.

Almost exactly ten years to the day after the Iron Blow was discovered, the Mt Lyell Railway was opened in 1896, and the treatment of Mt Lyell ores found to be a brilliant success. Total value of metals and minerals raised approached £1 million, out of which about £200 000 in dividends was paid exclusive of the first dividend of the Mt Lyell Mining and Railway Company. People and principles of sound government were trampled in the rush: the survey 'system' on the west coast silverfields was distinguished by applicants actually being permitted to employ their own surveyors to measure out Crown land. More significantly, the general manager of the Tasmanian Government Railways since March 1886, Frederick Back, counselled his political masters to be wary of over-enthusiasm and rashness when it came to mines because despite confident prediction, the general history of mining revealed that it was erratic and marked by a boom and bust cycle. He opposed sanctioning syndicate railways because they were detrimental to government railways and hence ultimately to all the people. He opposed fly-by-night mining entrepreneurs, some of whom had already distinguished themselves by floating bubble companies and were not above shooting fragments of gold into ore samples. Back repeatedly warned the government against sharing the common dementia and approving too many railways, and drew a parallel with overstocking a farm.

The main problem for the west coast mines was the lack of a suitable port. Macquarie Harbour was superb but the bar at the entrance prevented any ships but the smallest from entering. Thus it was that in 1897 C. Napier Bell was called to report on the prospect of deepening the entrance through Hell's Gates, adequate for convicts in the 1820s but not for exporting minerals in quantity and importing heavy machinery. The next year Bell concluded a precise report and recommendations for the construction of training walls and breakwaters so that vessels of up to 3000 tons might be admitted—though he could do nothing about the tremendous storms which battered the coast. Citing work done at Galveston in Texas and at the mouth of the Danube, Bell offered an estimate of nearly £200 000 to do the work. It was done.

In the financial year 1897–8, there was more legitimate mining activity in the colony than ever before. The amount of revenue was the largest since 1891 and the quantity of gold recovered turned out to be a record. More than 20 per cent of all mineral wealth came out of Mt Lyell though there was a decrease in silver production when buildings, machinery and mining plant were consumed in a bushfire during the summer of 1897–8. Some 4500 persons were by then engaged in mining, including a profitable tin mine at Lottah where electric light had been installed and an electric drill, probably the only one in Australia, was in use. The next year the number of miners had increased to more than 6000 as high prices for tin gave an impetus, so that the Tasmanian Dredging Company began active operations at Derby on the Ringarooma River.

At the end of the 1890s, few Tasmanians recognized the economy as having much relationship with that of twenty years earlier, save in the area of wool production and timber perhaps. By 1899, the population of the colony was 183 000, compared with 101 000 in 1870; the imports were £1.8 million (£790 000) and exports £2.6 million (£650 000). The part of minerals in this was: blister copper which amounted to £738 000; tin, £278 000; gold, £201 000; silver ore, £162 000. In other words, more than half the value of exports derived from four minerals.

Equally as striking was the distribution of these exports: the city of Launceston exported practically the same amount as Hobart, with Strahan very close behind; similar proportions applied to imports between the two cities.

As Launceston became wealthier so its civic pride increased. Much was made in 1892 of the jubilee year of the foundation of the Mechanics' Institute in March 1842, and attention freely drawn to the Institute and Public Library, as it was called, where in excess of 18 000 volumes, with reading rooms, were available to the public, and other rooms widely used by the industrious. There had been fostered in the north a love of works of art and the wonders of nature, from which was now sprung the Queen Victoria Museum and Art Gallery. The first annual report was presented in 1892, the whole splendid institution being opened by

Electric power station, Launceston, in the late nineteenth century the Governor in April 1891 in the presence of a large and brilliant assemblage. The subsequent conduct of visitors was noted as of the most exemplary character, as was only to be expected from the proud inhabitants of Launceston and its neighbourhood.

Buoyed up with enthusiasm in what Protestant zeal and enterprise might accomplish in the colony of Tasmania, northerners taking notice of proposals for the Melbourne Centennial Exhibition, promoted in 1885 a Launceston Exhibition also. Following this, and with a view to executing the proposal, the City Council was induced to undertake the erection of a hall in the City Park, to be named after the Queen's late consort, Prince Albert, at a cost of not less than £13 000. A Juvenile Industrial Exhibition was considered not ambitious enough and the scope was enlarged as Sir Edward Braddon, agent-general at the heart of the Empire, forwarded the work and secured exhibitors. Mr Jules Joubert's services were secured as director and then general manager early in 1891, and prior to its being closed in March 1892, the Exhibition was seen by no fewer than 262 000 people, children being encouraged to attend when offered nominal rail fares only. Lasting benefit of a moral, economic and ethical kind was thought to have been produced, despite the unfortunate onset of the depression.

In political terms the period of the 1890s was again distinguished by continual and persistent conflict between the two Houses of parliament. In August 1892, the government of Fysh was defeated after five years at the helm, and Henry Dobson became premier. As had been the case since the inauguration of self-government in 1856, the differences on the issues of the day were essentially those of whether to balance the budget by imposing taxes and/or raising fresh money by the issue of debentures. As the franchise ensured that members of parliament would more nearly represent all the people, though by no means all, the Legislative Council became more alert to detect any measures which might affect the class they represented, should threatening bills get through the House of Assembly. The conduct of the Council continued to reveal that it was composed of men whose ancestors would have opposed the invention of the wheel. Not that it was alone in offering a shining example of anti-democratic ideology and practice: in 1895, 1553 people had 3853 votes in the House of Assembly by the plural voting system. Of these, 1 had twelve votes, 1 had eleven, 4 had nine, 156 had three and 1,204 had two votes. In the Council, 735 voters accounted for 1682 votes; 1 had seven, 3 had six, 98 had three and 590 had two.

Still, it was a sign of the new liberal times that an act of 1891 made arrangements for payment of members of parliament, five years after a similar measure had finally been enacted in Victoria. A fixed sum of £100 a year was permitted for reimbursement in relation to attendance at parliament but this was reduced to £75 in 1893 as a result of the depression. Members also possessed free railway passes and free travel in their constituencies by mail conveyances, together with postal privileges during sessions.

Dobson's ministry at once set out to increase taxes by imposing liens on income and land, mortgages and probate. The Council opposed all this and the premier was granted a dissolution of parliament. All ministers were promptly re-elected, the premier and attorney-general without opposition. Sir Edward Braddon, late agent-general, now re-entered parliament and when Dobson's taxing measures continued to be rejected, the government resigned and Braddon became premier. His government came to office in April 1894.

As the depression continued, the Council consented to pass a Land Tax Bill but in mid-1894 still set its face against other measures which sought to raise a revenue, although financial necessities were all against it finally succeeding.

Drastic retrenchment was all the government could offer as the colonial debt increased, and a serious question arose concerning the connection of the late Treasurer (John Henry) with the Mt Lyell Co., and the premier with the Anchor Tin Mine Co. Braddon rode out the storm.

After this diversion, the Council continued to reject proposals for female suffrage but did at last come to a reluctant decision to permit a wider franchise for the House, though it struck out clauses which permitted the representation of minorities under the Hare system of counting votes by a species of proportional representation. However, it was finally agreed in 1896 at the instigation of Andrew Inglis Clark (a liberal who had a likeness of his hero Mazzini in every room) to redraw the boundaries of rural electorates, with one member of parliament each. Hobart was to be consolidated into one division of six members, to be elected by the new Hare system, with Launceston similarly made into a division returning four members, for one year to enable the

Timber industry in southern Tasmania, early twentieth century

new arrangements to have a trial. This complicated form of proportional representation was adopted throughout the state in 1907.

When ministers were returned, there were charges of improper
conduct in relation to the mining industry, Braddon being accused
of company-promoting when in England in 1896. Then Clark
resigned from the government, though observers were not sure
whether or not he had been made a scapegoat: his views were
certainly at variance with those of his colleagues on the extension
of railways. Clark became a member of the Opposition.

The economic tide continued to run strongly in Tasmania's
favour as timber exports boomed and the production at Mt Lyell
increased enormously with the new smelting process. To mark
this, members of parliament restored their salaries to £100 a year,
with ministers to receive £750, and some public servants who had
been retrenched were replaced. Braddon announced his retirement
because of ill-health: E. T. Miles, Minister for Lands and Works,
and the premier were both pronounced to have been implicated
in an improper tender for the Macquarie Harbour breakwater,
Miles being forced to resign. The Ministry of N. E. Lewis was

sworn in, just in time to make arrangements for the colony's contribution to the prosecution of the Boer War.

Tasmania had long been deeply interested in inter-colonial trade and reciprocity arrangements, owing to the lengthy period of economic depression and the colony's vulnerability to mainland tariffs. From 1883 it had been an enthusiastic member of the Federal Council, a body formed partly because of French and German presence in the south-west Pacific. Tasmania was particularly concerned, not least for historical reasons, about French transportation of convicts to the area. The Federal Council of recent years had accomplished little, however, except the provision of holidays for the delegates. Indeed, at the fourth meeting in January 1891, only Queensland, Victoria and Tasmania sent representatives.

In such areas as literature and sport, however, there was a growing sense of nationalism and, probably equally as important, the realization that a free trade zone was certainly in the interests of many colonists and business concerns. An Australian Economic Community was called for. The examples of unification in Germany and Italy appeared to illustrate that the formation of nation-states was in the logic of history, and differing tariffs became a more significant irritant as the colonies grew and prospered and internal markets for secondary products assumed greater importance.

With no executive power or revenue of its own, and no machinery to compel colonies to join, the Federal Council was not a great unifying force but the impulse for federation gathered strength. It was given a most substantial boost by a report on defence prepared by Major General Sir Bevan Edwards, an imperial officer who did not mince matters. The armed forces of the colonies would do well to combine, he warned. His voice had the impact of authority and opinion emanating from the seat of the empire in London, and it was heeded.

Against this background, and with foreknowledge of Edwards' report which was shortly to be released, Sir Henry Parkes at Tenterfield made a passionate plea for federation, and all colonies, including New Zealand, were impressed enough to send delegates to an Australasian conference at Melbourne in 1890. Tasmania was represented by Andrew Inglis Clark and B. Stafford Bird.

Clark was particularly important in the federation movement.

A lawyer born in Hobart Town in 1848, he became deeply impressed by the American Constitution and republican ideals and was a Tasmanian delegate to the Federal Council from 1888. Then prior to the Australian Convention summoned in 1891, he circulated to interested parties his own draft constitution bill, a document which greatly assisted to direct the thoughts of the drafting committee.

Bird, the other Tasmanian, was an English-born Methodist clergyman and subsequently farmer, and interested in finance. From 1894 to 1897 he was Speaker of the House of Assembly, and treasurer from 1899 to 1903.

In 1891 a form of written Constitution was hammered out, basically the one which was to be adopted as the Constitution of the Commonwealth of Australia. The colonies, however, found many difficulties in surrendering part of their independence and the move to federation was impeded especially by the attitude of New South Wales, where Parkes was defeated in an election. Then in 1893 a conference at Corowa recommended that each of the colonies elect representatives by popular vote to forward the work of federation. Two years later, in Hobart, the premiers approved the Corowa resolutions and recommended that each colony elect ten representatives.

The Tasmanians were P. O. Fysh, N. J. Brown, Adye Douglas, William Moore, Sir Edward Braddon, Neil Lewis, John Henry, Charles Grant, Henry Dobson and Matthew Clarke, all except Clarke members of the current government or the most recent one. Andrew Inglis Clark did not stand and Bird was defeated.

All premiers and certain other colonists joined the elected men and a total of seventy-nine began their deliberations, sitting on and off for twelve months. A great deal of labour was spent on the compromise which would be necessary to prevent the two most populous colonies from utterly dominating the proposed union and to preserve as many colonial rights as was consistent with a wish for federation.

A popular vote on federation was taken on 3 June 1898, though Queensland stood aloof and so did Western Australia, recently catapulted by gold discoveries from a Crown colony to one enjoying self-government. The key colony was New South Wales which reflected its seniority, economic independence and fear of losing sovereignty by laying down that at least 80 000 voters must support a 'Yes' vote for it to be committed to a federation. This figure was not reached when 71 595 voted for the federation and 68 228 against.

On the other hand, Victoria and South Australia voted in favour of the proposal by majorities of five to one and two to one respectively. In Tasmania there was a huge majority of 11 797 to 2716 in favour, nearly 50 per cent of electors on the roll casting a vote. Indeed, the 'Yes' votes amounted to no less than 81 per cent of formal votes. Of the twenty-nine electorates, twenty-five voted in favour of the federation, the four which did not being all in the Midlands or on the East coast. There was also a hefty 30 per cent 'No' vote from Hobart, in marked comparison to the high affirmative opinion of Launceston where no anti-federation meetings at all were reported. It may be that the influence of the *Mercury* was felt when it counselled caution until the financial implications were clarified, and B. S. Bird also voiced a doubt, producing statistics to show that Tasmania would lose financially under the proposed form of union.

The voice of labour as it found expression in the pages of the *Clipper* was similar to that of the *Bulletin* and the *Tocsin*, emphasizing what was described as the undemocratic nature of the proposed federation in terms of the powers to be given to the Senate. But it was difficult to sway Tasmanians on the basis of such ideological considerations. It was not so difficult to cast doubt on the financial implications for the future and it was urged that the contemplated tariff simply would not be adequate to return to the island a sum equal to that surrendered by passing control of customs and excise to a central authority. Even the enthusiastic federalist A. I. Clark was uneasy on the point and declined publicly to support the 'Yes' campaign, choosing to remain silent.

R. M. Johnston, the government statistician, was convinced that the new Tasmanian state would go broke if its income from customs duties and tariffs were removed, predicting that the people would be obliged to depend on federal largesse. It was pointed out that whereas Tasmania derived 44 per cent of its entire government income from duties levied on imports, New South Wales received only 17 per cent from that source, Victoria 31 per cent, South Australia 22 per cent and even Western Australia 38 per cent. In these circumstances it was feared that Tasmania would be forced to obtain from its residents a considerably larger amount by direct taxation than would be the case with other colonies.

As Johnston perceived the matter, the proposal financial arrangements would mean that the smaller states would be compelled to come cap in hand to the federal government for handouts, thus being reduced to beggars or poor relations in a federation which they were being told would shower down blessings upon them. He was right, but such fears were confused by a mass of differing tables of figures, and the plain man rendered uncertain. The Australian Natives' Association and such as the Colonial Treasurer, P. O. Fysh, tried to allay concern by asserting that no one in his right mind should expect perfection in an imperfect world, and he pleaded for people to take the long view and be optimistic. To this note of sweet reason, Fysh added a telling point—if Tasmania refused to accept entry into the federation on the proffered terms of equality with other colonies, then it might be forced to accept less palatable terms later on. Tasmania was too small and insignificant in the Australian context to throw its weight about like New South Wales or demand changes to finance which had been arrived at only after tedious, complicated and laborious exertions by the delegates and their advisers.

As was clear, the Australian colonies bore no resemblance to the American colonies represented at Philadelphia a century and more previously. There was no sense of Australia being powerfully propelled into nationhood, no sense of outraged urgency or arrogant imperial authority, no democratic ideology being debated, and certainly no sense of nationality sealed with the blood of martyrs. Whereas the American patriots began the document which enshrined their hopes with a ringing cry that all men were created equal and had certain inalienable rights, the Australian colonists began their document with three paragraphs humbly deferring to Great Britain and Queen Victoria.

When fewer than the required number of 'Yes' voters cast a 'Yes' ballot in New South Wales, it appeared that the federal cause had suffered a substantial setback but this difficulty was quickly overcome. Most importantly, there was an election scheduled in the colony, and the fact that there had been a small overall majority in favour of federation called for political decision. After some consultations, the New South Wales premier Reid found himself able to recommend a new Enabling Act. On 20 June 1899 the crucial support of the voters of New South Wales was secured for federation, and when Western Australia threw in its lot with the other colonies, the final steps in the creation of the Commonwealth of Australia could be taken by the imperial parliament. In

Loyalty

Tasmania, opposition to federation this second time round had dwindled to a tiny 791 votes.

As the voting revealed, it was unthinkable that Tasmania could or would stand aside from the federal movement. There were risks indeed, but they were uncertain and the subject of dispute among eminent authorities, whereas the advantages of being part of a larger whole would surely outweigh them. The final opinion of Tasmanians was summed up in the mixture of motive and metaphor expressed by a local orator who said that if the people of the island voted for federation they would establish a great and glorious nation under the bright Southern Cross, and meat would be cheaper; that they would survive to see the day when the Australian race dominated the southern seas and at the same time have a market for their potatoes and apples; and that their sons would reap the grand heritage of nationhood.

There was still the prospect of the majority of Australians having the majority of votes in parliamentary elections, but this tyranny of the majority was diminished for Tasmania and the smaller colonies by the arrangements for a Senate which was to give each colony the same number of representatives no matter how huge or tiny it was. Alfred Deakin perceived that such a House would not · in practice represent the states, but party interests instead. However that would be, now there were called into existence fourteen houses of parliament to govern fewer than four million people.

Thus was a price paid for the creation of the Commonwealth of Australia. It was without avail that some protested at the embodiment of essentially anti-democratic sentiments and a state of things designed to perpetuate conflicts and demarcation disputes and inefficiency as the result of conflict between state and federal authorities, with the taxpayer to meet the costs, feather the nests of constitutional lawyers and create a vast and overlapping bureaucracy.

5

Entanglement

Deep loyalty to the Empire in the case of Tasmania continued to flourish and was reinforced by the tiny size of the colony, its distance from the metropolitan authority and its consequent exposed position in the event of war. Periodic invasion scares had for almost a century galvanized the colonists into seeing to their defences, especially those of Hobart.

In June 1897 there came an opportunity to demonstrate fervent patriotism when celebrations of Queen Victoria's Diamond Jubilee occupied the greater part of a week. The mayor of Hobart presented commemoration medals to 5000 children who sang the National Anthem, and in the afternoon gave a free dinner to the poor, an occasion of charity lent depth of purpose by the presence of the governor. At 10 p.m. at the Town Hall a huge crowd sang a hymn of praise at the precise hour of the thanksgiving service conducted in faraway St Paul's. The personal message from Her Majesty and the governor's loyal response was read out from the Town Hall balcony, and there was an outburst of cheers. To mark the great occasions, various charitable schemes were set on foot in deference to the known wishes of the old Queen.

For many years volunteer forces, small in number but enthusiastic, had carried on against government and public indifference but there now emerged the first serious chance to give the wider world a palpable demonstration of the island colony's eagerness to leap into action should the Empire be threatened. The opportunity arose when war began between the Boer republics in South Africa and Britain in October 1899.

The move to war had been evident for some time, and four days before the outbreak and three days after Western Australia and South Australia introduced legislation to send contingents, Tasmania also cabled offering colonial infantry. A bill was then passed through both houses of parliament upon the motion of Braddon, authorizing the expenditure of £4500 on equipment for eighty men, a fine body of soldiers drawn from all parts of the colony. Commanding them was Captain Cyril Cameron, an experienced imperial soldier who, following the ever-glorious and historic march from Kabul, had been present at the relief of Kandahar under Lord Roberts.

Scenes of both impressive imperial sentiment and local pride were witnessed as the contingent prepared to depart from Tasmania. In Hobart the administrator, in addressing the men, stressed the proof offered of their devotion to Queen and Empire. He emphasized that England had been forced into a quarrel but that the insignificant authors of a turbulent rising could not yelp at the British flag without chastisement. The Queen's message was then read out to the respectful throng: 'Her Majesty the Queen desires to thank the people of Tasmania for their striking manifestation of loyalty and patriotism in their voluntary offer to send troops to co-operate with Her Majesty's Imperial Forces in maintaining her position and the rights of British subjects in South Africa. She wishes the troops God-speed and a safe return.'

Mrs Dodds, wife of the administrator, then presented a silver bugle to Captain Cameron. She said, 'It gives me great pleasure to present to you this silver bugle.' Members of the contingent were then marched to the Temperance Hall where a reception was given by the mayoress, Mrs J. G. Davies, assisted by the mayor (Lieutenant-Colonel C. E. Davies), in uniform, and Miss Davies. Among those present were several relatives of the men, some of whom were moved to tears. The recruits wore khaki uniforms. Mr T. Julian Haywood, the city organist, presided at the piano.

At the later Town Hall banquet toasts were drunk to 'Her Majesty the Queen' and 'The Contingent'. The crowd joined in singing the National Anthem and 'Soldiers of the Queen'. Mr A. D. Watchorn rendered 'The Gallants of England' and the Chorus from McKenzie's 'Jubilee Ode' was sung by the Philharmonic Society, under the baton of Mr Arundel Orchard. The men left for the Barracks to the strains of 'Rule Britannia' and 'Auld Lang Syne'. On the 27th, the recruits left Launceston, the greatest enthusiasm prevailing both there and in Hobart.

Following the disasters of 'Black Week' in South Africa and the unexpected news that the Afrikaner forces were more formidable than had been supposed, a further contingent of forty-five men was organized to leave Tasmania in February 1900, selected from three times that number of Volunteers. This contingent was followed by another in early March, a group necessarily quite untrained and undisciplined but capable of riding and shooting well.

Each morning, newspaper offices were surrounded by crowds seeking war news, and telegrams posted outside were eagerly read by all classes. Hobart was decked with flags to mark the British column entering Kimberley and the capture of General Cronje, but those manifestations of delight were completely over-shadowed when Ladysmith was relieved. As the result of prior arrangement, the news was announced by firing five guns from the battery between 1 and 2 a.m., at which the population turned out and sang patriotic songs all the rest of the night. Next day there was a stirring demonstration at the Town Hall and a general holiday, with scarcely a person not wearing a tricolour badge or rosette.

The proposal from the mainland colonies to form a regiment of mounted infantry about 1000 strong, from all Australia, was responded to warmly in Tasmania and fifty men and fifty-five horses embarked for the veldt. In December 1899 a patriotic fund opened and £7000 was collected. Among the ladies of the colony there was formed a Union Jack Society (President, Lady Gormanston) to send warm clothing and comforts to the men at the front.

The Boer War was marked by other exciting scenes than the embarkation of soldiers. In March 1900 James Paton stood for parliament, the first aspirant to come forward in the labour interest. He was editor and proprietor of the *Clipper*, judged by the governor as low-class and pro-Boer. Paton got W. A. Holman from New South Wales to lecture on the subject of the war in South Africa, with the newspaperman in the chair. But when Holman began to speak and to cast doubts on the lily-white motives of Britain, he was dragged from the platform by some of the audience and roughly handled while Paton took refuge under a table and then escaped. Paton withdrew from the parliamentary contest.

Although the relief of Mafeking was celebrated with enormous enthusiasm, the role of the Australian forces in Kitchener's campaign against the guerillas, together with the confusion and shame caused by the execution of 'Breaker' Morant, removed much of the glitter which had marked the war in its early stages. Tasmanians, together with their fellow-Australians in the new federation, were obliged to wait for the fulfilment of their lust for recognition as warriors and true-blue sons of the Empire on which the sun never set.

Still, the jam-makers Jones and Company and Moore and Company, of Hobart, secured sales (1.616 million tins) of their product to the British military forces through the enterprise of the agent-general in London, Alfred Dobson. Jam-making and fruit production began to go from strength to strength in the Edwardian era, though after losing £4000 in one season, Messrs Knight and Company retired from business and in 1912 W. D. Peacock recorded that Henry Jones himself was so discouraged that he offered to sell his interest in the trade to Peacock for £100, which that gentleman refused.

The growth and confidence of Tasmania was not really tested in the early years of the century, for general prosperity and the work of Braddon in the constitutional conventions led to Tasmania being sheltered from the impact of free trade by the introduction of section 87 ('Braddon's Blot') whereby three-quarters of the revenue from customs and excise was to be returned to the states for ten years.

Education of the young continued to be poor. Fees were paid on an irregular basis, the situation of many teachers was wretched in terms of income and conditions, the curricula were character-ized by lack of imagination, and attendance at school was very low. There was an annual enrolment of 23 000 at the state schools, an average attendance of 17 000, and 3000 children of school age did not attend at all—so it was computed in 1899 when many schools were closed by epidemics. Even this was a doubtful figure because some children not attending state schools were claimed by their parents to be attending private schools, a fact which could not be really checked because such schools were not obliged to show inspectors anything except their formal registers. Income of teachers was principally (64 per cent) between £70 and £150, with 21 per cent on salaries between £150 and £300. Women teachers were on substantially lower salaries than males. and no females were in the £150–£400 category, though sixty men were.

Strawberry jam label for Jones & Co. in the late nineteenth century

Design sought for jam tins

There also existed the practice of awarding Exhibitions, begun in 1860 and continued for thirty-four years. These were tenable at private schools recognized by the Board of Education as 'superior schools', and there existed the belief or assurance that teachers were able and willing to educate exhibitioners up to the Associate of Arts degree.

A problem with this system was that most candidates came from a very small minority of schools and that the offer of Exhibitions was valueless as a stimulus to improvement in the work of schools generally. There were those educationists who argued that the money would be better spent on free primary education for all instead of free secondary education for the select few.

In 1900 there came the retirement of James Rule who had spent forty-four years as a Tasmanian teacher, inspector and then Director of Education and forty of those years working unsuccessfully for the abolition of the school fees system. He was enabled to report that in the 1890s the number of schools increased from 240 to 309, gross enrolment from 18 000 to 23 000, expenditure from public funds from £33 000 to £40 000, and school fees from £10 000 to £11 000. Side by side with the colonial schools were 241 private ones, with an enrolment of about 9000 pupils, 4000 in Hobart and 3000 in Launceston.

But the abolition of fees was in the air, though B. Stafford Bird, treasurer in the Lewis ministry, warned that it would cost about £15 000 in new taxation. Perhaps it was not worth it: a new inspector of schools in the early 1900s reported sourly that Reading was too often taught in such a way that it led to a monotonous sing-song intonation; that History consisted usually of a string of dates and names of sovereigns, whereas a well-told story of a gallant deed or a description of the doings of the Empire's great men in the brave old days of old was of infinitely more interest and service to the children than any bald record of events or columns of figures, while the flushed cheeks, kindling eyes and rapt attention of his listeners would be a very sufficient reward to the teacher of History for his preparation; that in Drill the children were well trained in a few cases but in some instances the movement of the pupils being drilled presented a truly melancholy spectacle; but that in Singing, even when there was little more than a hideous medley of sound being produced, the pupils appeared thoroughly to enjoy it.

By the end of 1900, teachers had their full salaries paid by the

Education Department, with school fees collected and paid into the government revenue, and the educational standard of the teachers raised. Most importantly, in 1904 W. L. Neale, of the South Australian Education Department, was appointed to look into the entire system of primary education in the state and, following his report, he was appointed director. Neale's findings and recommendations ushered in reforms in classification of schools and teachers, increase of salaries, teacher training and school inspection, new school buildings and the introduction of a new curriculum and improved methods of teaching.

Then in 1906 an act was passed to register all schools and teachers, and as a result some interesting data were gathered on the private schools, the more disreputable of which were obliged to close their doors. To the astonishment of no one who studied the education of young Tasmanians, it was found that 36 per cent of all children aged between six and fourteen were not on any school roll. This was largely because city schools were perfectly inadequate and the compulsory attendance provided under the legislation was a farce. Strenuous efforts were subsequently made to enforce attendance at school.

The same year a training college was established at Hobart, complete with a scheme of scholarships to encourage those who might otherwise have been unable to advance themselves, and finally free education was achieved in 1908.

The regime of Neale led to a great deal of discontent among teachers and a series of enquiries was instituted. The upshot of this was a 1909 report which ventured to suggest that the administration of the Department under Neale had been irregular and that Neale's lack of tact in dealing with some of his teachers had greatly irritated certain of their number. Some were convinced that teachers brought from South Australia received favoured treatment. Neale was praised for his high ideals, zeal and untiring industry in bringing Tasmanian education into the twentieth century, but his services were dispensed with. Such was the fate of a reformer at the hands of his opponents and, it would appear, less than competent administrators.

New regulations, however, were framed and more power in the way of promoting children from one grade to another placed in the hands of the teacher and less in the hands of the inspector, who was relieved of the task of mark-giving. In 1911 the Philip Smith

W. L. Neale, Director of Education 1904–9

Training College for teachers, established through the generosity of a wealthy landholder, was opened in Hobart on the Domain, adjacent to the University, which had taken over the old Hobart High School buildings.

Then in 1913 State High Schools were first established at Hobart and Launceston and courses organized for those who wished to go on to university, those who sought to teach, those who wished to take up a commercial career, those who would become tradesmen and those girls who required to be fitted for home duties, according to the custom of the time. Exams were conducted at the end of the second and fourth year, and entrance to the High School provided for by a qualifying exam set by the Education Department which in 1912 raised the compulsory school-leaving age from thirteen to fourteen years.

In 1915 arrangements were made for junior and senior bursaries to be awarded, with special attention paid to children who dwelt in the country, and at the same time two more High Schools, to the intermediate level, were established at Burnie and Devonport. In 1918, a Technical Education branch took over the conduct of all technical schools and schools of mines.

When federation was accomplished in 1901, the government of Tasmania was in the hands of N. E. Lewis's administration, the Braddon ministry having fallen after the shocks of the Strahan Marine Board scandals. If there was a prevailing political ideology in the new state, it was not easily to be distinguished from a general 'for the good of the colony' vagueness which was invoked when seeking votes in terms of 'development'. A form of confused liberalism, however, had emerged and there was also the beginning of a labour form of liberalism. Tasmanians were well aware of political developments elsewhere, especially in Victoria, but the trade union movement in the island was small both in numbers and in impact, not least because the west coast mining boom was geographically utterly isolated from the other main centres of population in the state; the area of mining population was in fact as readily accessible by sea from Victoria as from Hobart. Most importantly, the Legislative Council continued to exist basically unreformed, unrepentant and unyielding to criticism. The fact that it did not represent the people of the state as a whole was regarded by the Council as a virtue and as a powerful argument for its supreme political power. Its continued flaunting of control of the legislative process for the sake of 'interests' remained a permanent problem to every member of the House of Assembly, even if he were elected from constituencies which did not include all adults. This was corrected when, as one result of federation and its franchise, women received the vote. The powerful presence of the Council was and continued to be one of the most important political factors in Tasmania. But there was another.

This was the rise of the labour movement and the establishment of a Labor party. In 1900, James Paton of the *Clipper*, launched in 1893, had stood in the general interests of labour for the Democratic League but was obliged to withdraw after the physical attacks on himself and Holman, and accusations by an angry *Mercury* that he was not loyal. This was enough in a period when the theatre put on *British Born* and *Briton or Boer*, when local horses were named 'Bobs', after Lord Roberts, and 'Britisher', and the Tasmanian soldiers at the front identified as 'Tommies'. To support labour in any form was essentially anti-British during the Boer War, with the *Clipper* offering biting sarcasm about the visit of royalty in 1901. For the people of a free democracy there was a galling nameless insult in the gaze of a typical British aristocrat, perceived the paper, and in the splendour of that gaze Hobart snobs, it was observed, grovelled happily all the week.

The election of the colourful King O'Malley to federal parliament for an electorate dominated by west coast miners revealed that much might be done by labour forces, though the level of commitment to 'Labour' by miners was marginal, and the coherence of O'Malley that of a shrewd showman. He was a master of publicity stunts and said to have held the largest meeting ever seen in the important silver town of Zeehan in 1901. He allegedly sued a Launceston clergyman when an earthquake, prayed for to teach sinners in the congregation a lesson, actually eventuated, and also was said to have put up the Earth for sale. He variously offered to run the Australian Capital Territory, a ministry of insurance, the Commonwealth Bank (with or without pay) until it was properly started, Australia's defences in preference to importing British officers, and the British Empire. He also observed that parliament was the only institution in the country which was operated by unskilled labour and stated that all the powers-that-be in Tasmania were corrupt. This sort of thing went down very well in some quarters, and O'Malley naturally attracted supporters.

Following the federal elections, the interests of labour received a certain amount of stimulation, especially on the west coast. A Political Labour League was formed, and when Lewis's ministry was defeated after it too tried to introduce income tax, three Labor candidates were successful. These were J. J. Long (Lyell), G. M. Burns (Queenstown) and W. Lamerton (Zeehan). Crosby Gilmore (Waratah) supported Labor but not the Labor pledge. As one result, the Mt Lyell Company sacked Long for daring to be political to the point of winning a seat in parliament, and did not look favourably on other Labor men.

An important factor in arousing the voters to a consciousness of the labour interest was the *Clipper*, taken over by W. A. Woods after Paton was ruined by libel cases, and dedicated to the political education of Tasmanians, especially in relation to the land monopolies said to sustain sinister reactionary forces. The 1903 election could not be regarded as a triumph for Labor. The association between the Labor members and the trade union movement, such as it was, remained equivocal and uncertain and the election was in fact a great victory for W. B. Propsting, who became premier in April. He had offered a liberal programme which, as elsewhere in Australia, included many of the points advocated by Labor, such as old-age pensions, land value taxation and compulsory purchase by the government of certain large properties for closer settlement.

The cry was often heard that Tasmania could never advance until such old estates, thought frequently to have been granted to magnates in the convict era, were purchased and 'developed'. The *Clipper* especially said this, giving space to the ideas of A. J. Ogilvy who tirelessly argued for land taxes and land resumption but to no avail while the Legislative Council remained in situ. In parliament, when Woods moved for the Council's abolition, only the Labor men supported him, the Liberals shrinking from taking such a radical step.

Propsting's administration survived barely twelve months because he was at once confronted with an antagonistic Council which regarded him and his programme as wicked, evil and immoral. Defeated, he was succeeded by J. W. Evans, Propsting himself securing a seat in the Council and then, to cap it all, becoming a minister in Evans's government. As the *Daily Post* commented brightly, when the faithful clubbed together to send Propsting as a missionary to the Legislative Council to convert and reform, it would have been wiser had they simply clubbed Propsting. It is difficult to imagine a more telling example of the political scene among non-Labor groups in the state.

Subsequently the Liberals and Labor tended to run in double harness, as at the federal level, but Labor's task of educating the people to vote for it went forward at snail's pace; in 1905, Labor supporters were estimated at 2000 only and trade unionists at merely 1500. In these circumstances, the work of the controversial and radical Anglican bishop J. E. Mercer and the ex-Presbyterian cleric John Palamountain became important as did the visits of mainland Labor men such as J. C. Watson, W. G. Spence and Frank Anstey, who conducted consciousness-raising sessions.

In 1906, seven Labor men were successful in a House of thirty-five and began to trouble such supporters of caution as the *Mercury*. The extraordinary conduct of Propsting did great harm to the Liberal cause and the workers began to consider that support for Labor was quite possibly in their interests. Leader of the party was John Earle, whose power base on the west coast was broader than that of the more intellectual Woods about whom there clung an odour of scandal: he was not Tasmanian-born, he had travelled a lot, he had changed his name, and he was suspected of embezzlement. In addition, Earle was supported by a coterie of able men centred about L. F. Giblin. Their influence may have been decisive. Others thought it fatal to the development of an intellectually adventurous Labor ideology. The *Clipper* was most important in Tasmania: it was the only paper to foster a working-class sense of identity, to try to reach out to the small farmers, and to urge women to vote Labor. At a time when the *Mercury* omitted or misreported Labor news, the *Clipper* gave information on the franchise, reminded people to enrol, raised funds and so on.

In 1909, J. A. Lyons was first elected to state parliament for the House, after being a teacher irritated by the administration of Neale's Education Department, and was one of twelve Labor men in a House of thirty members (reduced from thirty-five), elected under the Hare–Clarke system and composed of five six-member

J. A. Lyons, premier of Tasmania (1923–8) and later Prime Minister of Australia

electorates. Labor had won two out of six seats in every electorate except Darwin, which included the west coast, where it won four.

Among those prominent in the onslaught on Neale had been N. K. Ewing, a very able and ambitious lawyer who represented the teachers, and his political objects were temporarily satisfied when his election to the House in 1909 led to the defeat of the Evans government at the hands of an alliance between Labor and a Liberal League—but when Earle became Labor premier, his opponents realized what they had done and brought him down, so that Lewis was reinstated and Labor cast back from whence it had so impertinently arisen.

Woods and David Balchen commenced to form the Workers'

Political League in 1907, when Woods became editor of the *Clipper*, and the party continued to gain strength in Tasmania as it did on the mainland, and to represent a wider cross-section of the people. The admirably cheeky *Clipper*, sustaining a lethal blow by losing a libel action, was replaced in 1910 by the *Daily Post* as the voice of labour; the latter secured the services of Edmund Dwyer-Gray, member of a distinguished Irish literary family associated with the Dublin *Freeman's Journal* and Parnell. Under Dwyer-Gray, the *Daily Post* perceived socialism as the peak of human progress, Tasmania having only reached a stage somewhere between feudalism and wage slavery. Dwyer-Gray regarded the Legislative Council not so much as a lion in the path of progress, as a stuffed donkey. This body, said the *Daily Post* bravely, regarded Tasmania's colonial constitution as if it were a revelation brought down from Mt Wellington by a modern Moses.

But the socialist objective of Labor was not adopted in Tasmania, partly as a result of the pragmatism of the Australian Workers' Union, partly because Tasmanian workers had been cowed, defeated and knocked about for so long at the hands of their strong opponents, because industrial trade unionism lacked the cutting edge of ideology it received elsewhere, and partly because intellectual Labor men such as Giblin and W. E. Shoobridge were really more liberal than anything else.

The federal election of 1910 put Labor into office at the national level and was a huge encouragement to the movement in Tasmania. It was only a question of time, exulted supporters, before Tasmania had its first Labor government. This was aided by the establishment of wages boards in 1910 and, the same year, a carters' and drivers' strike which paralysed Hobart when the men struck work for £2 instead of £1.10s. for a 56-hour week.

Under the Hare–Clark system of voting, in 1912 Labor secured fourteen of the thirty seats in the House of Assembly. Labor publicists maintained that every kind of lie had been told about Labor and thousands of pounds spent by the anti-Labor forces to keep the party out of office.

Labor's accession to power in the House finally came in 1914 in a curious way and was largely the result of potatoes. One J. T. H. Whitsitt defected from the Solomon government because he was not satisfied that enough had been done to induce mainland states, fearing the Irish blight, to accept Tasmanian potatoes; in 1911 nearly all crops of the old Redskin variety were destroyed, and replaced by the blight-resistant Brownell for export to New South Wales. At the same time as the eccentric Irishman Whitsitt stood by the potato, a by-election in Denison was won by Labor and it secured office, although the governor did his level best to place conditions on the appointment of Earle as premier, and was subsequently rebuked by London.

Thus Labor, with Woods as Speaker, depended on Whitsitt and, of course, had no representative in the Legislative Council, the members of which could thereby claim that when they annihilated Labor bills they were dutifully reflecting the equivocal claim the party had to the House of Assembly.

The new government was not in power and gravely hindered in office. Nevertheless, it managed some quite important reforms. Earle, earlier denounced as pro-Boer and blacklisted by some mine managers, soon followed the path of Hughes and Holman and was drawn further by the tentacles of respectability and responsibility to the Right. It was a measure of this that the *Mercury* likened his policy speech in July 1914 to that of a Liberal, an unassailable argument that Earle had parted company with Labor ideology as it had been perceived by such as the *Clipper* and *Daily Post*. Earle struck a note frequently to be heard from Labor in Tasmania: he spoke heavily of 'justice' for all sections of the community, without considering that some sections might already have their share, and more.

W. H. Lee became Liberal leader in 1915 and during that year and 1916 the question of conscription for the war became ever hotter with the conduct of the Prime Minister, W. M. Hughes, in England and, probably most importantly of all, the catastrophic losses sustained by the AIF at Fromelles and on the Somme during that dreadful (northern) summer when the Australian infantry was chopped to pieces in the onsets launched by Haig and resisted to the last foot by the German army. Some 27 000 Australian soldiers were lost on three miles of ridge east of Amiens in about ten weeks, the ground was literally soaked with the blood of sons of the Empire, and Australia began to bleed to death. So it was that a struggle beyond imagination was to lead to the destruction of the Labor party in Australia. When W. M. Hughes agreed to ask the people whether or not they wanted conscription for overseas

Dame Enid Lyons on her wedding day, 1915

service, he virtually single-handedly tore down the party he had done so much to construct, revealing the strength of his attachment to Empire and the weakness of his association with those in the Labor party who had grave reservations about Hughes and his cronies.

But meanwhile in the first year of the conflict in Europe, the party did well enough in Tasmania. All that could be done was done to succour the mining industry which had been so dependent on German markets; Ewing, leader of the Liberals at the time, undertook to offer all reasonable support to the government in the crisis. The Legislative Council, however, reacted sharply when Labor sought to take action against war profiteers, and threw out no fewer than seven bills passed by the House. Then Labor failed to make headway in by-elections and the Council took a savage axe to a Lyons budget when the treasurer attempted to redistribute wealth along the lines pioneered by Lloyd George in England. Earle upset many when he refused to grant preference for trade union members on the grounds that it was sectional, and the Labor movement began to split, as elsewhere in Australia, on the subject of labour policy versus the defeat of Germany—as if the one could not be accomplished without the other. A proposed truce with the Liberals came to nothing and in the election of 1916 the Liberals won narrowly because Labor had been unable to deliver and had been seen to shilly-shally.

One of the most significant things done during the first year of the war was the government's takeover of the production of hydro-electricity. In 1891 the sudden prospect of substantial mining development on the west coast, especially that related to the silver discoveries at Mt Zeehan, induced John Coates and Company of Melbourne to look into the construction of gas and electric works, and at the same time, by the Australasian Rights Purchase Bill, electric works were foreshadowed on and near the Henty River, on the west coast. The Australasian Rights Purchase Association was then taken over by the Tasmanian Water Power Electric Company in 1892, which in turn let a contract for a track to be cut from Zeehan to the Pieman, but it took too long and there was a dispute.

In 1895 it was proposed to erect works at a spot near the junction of the Pieman and Heemskirk rivers, to generate electricity to supply light and power to Zeehan, the falls for motive power being 150 feet high. But it was predicted that there would be difficulties in the summer unless storage reservoirs were built, and so the scheme was abandoned though a fine waterpower was obtainable there. The same year, there was a Hobart Gas Company Electric Light Bill canvassed, with interested parties citing examples from North America and Europe.

The great attraction for persons interested in supplying electric power was Zeehan, where in 1896 there was recorded a proposal to erect steam works to supply electricity, the people becoming irritated by being forced to use kerosene. More than that, the cost of firewood for the boilers at the Silver Queen mine nearly doubled to supply the power needed for light, pumps and the town, which had at least nineteen hotels, it was asserted, of which Clarke's boasted sixty or seventy rooms. Meanwhile electricity was being harnessed at the Lottah tin mines, near the Blue Tier, in the north-east, but the original Zeehan scheme came to nothing at that time.

In these circumstances, a Zeehan Electric Light and Power Bill (1898) was canvassed with P. J. E. Fowler, a newspaper proprietor, the leading light as it were. There was by then an electric plant at the Silver Queen mine and Fowler proposed to generate electricity by steam, and was strongly supported by A. Morrisby, chairman of the town board. He drew attention to the dark and hazardous state of the streets and the danger of kerosene causing fires, so that insurance rates ran as high as £5 per £100, with 600 cases of kerosene consumed every month. By 1900 the Zeehan Electric Light and Power Company had a lease for its site and commenced construction of a station building, and soon Zeehan became the first town outside Launceston and Hobart to have electricity.

In 1895 the energetic northern city characteristically took the initiative and became the first city in the southern world to be connected with the new electric light: Launceston City Council harnessed the waters of the South Esk in December 1895 and generated 600 horsepower at the Duck Reach power station, with arc lamps studding the principal streets. In 1911 the Hydro-Electric and Metallurgical Company at the Great Lake started works to generate power at Waddamana for the treatment of ores by electrolytic methods, and three years later these assets were bought by the state when a bill was passed in August 1914.

Thus came into being the Hydro-Electric Department, which by 1916 had installed generators at Waddamana to create power for domestic lighting and trams in Hobart. After nearly five years, then, the Great Lake power scheme came into operation, with Mt Lyell ready to take its 20 000 horsepower within eighteen months.

At the same time as these technological changes were ushering Tasmania into the twentieth century, however, the system of alliances constructed in Europe and the nationalistic ambitions of parts of the Austro-Hungarian Empire proved a fatal combination. When Germany invaded Belgium in an attempt to neutralize or defeat France, Britain was drawn into the continental conflict and the arrival of Armageddon was signalled on 4 August 1914 when war was declared.

The outbreak of the Great War was greeted in Tasmania, as elsewhere in Australia, with protestations of loyalty to Britain and the Empire as had been the case with the outbreak of the Boer War. But in the Edwardian period a considerable amount of material was produced to make Germans offensive to true-blue Britons; the Kaiser had upset Britain by his attitude to the Boer conflict and generally Germany was recognized as an economic rival to the British Empire. Thus people with names which might be of German origin were at once persecuted and Tasmania no less than anywhere else offered abundant evidence for a study of the pathology of racism. This was made worse by the distress in the mines and outcries from people who earned a living trapping wallabies, rabbits and so on because one of their markets had been Leipzig, now cut off.

In 1916 the question was decided of whether the hotels should close at 6 p.m. or 10 p.m. (the government had already reduced closing time from 11.30 p.m. to 10 p.m.), the drink question to be resolved by conducting a plebiscite (mistakenly termed a 'referendum'). The case for moderation, if not prohibition, was immeasurably strengthened by the sobering news that his Majesty the King had let it be known he would abstain from alcoholic liquor, except for medicinal purposes, for the duration of the war. The conflict was obviously serious and the point was underlined further, were that possible, when the staff of the University of Melbourne also stated they would abstain.

The Tasmanians voted for 6 o'clock closing, the liquor trade finding it very difficult to muster a good argument against the

King. This vote was conducted at the same time as the state election in which Labor was defeated, and it was a measure of the political differences perceived between Labor under Earle and the Liberals, that some paid more attention to the liquor question than to the election.

A month later the first Anzac Day in Tasmania was commemorated with enormous emotion, as elsewhere in Australia and in London. Imperial feeling and Australian patriotic sentiment existing easily within it reached the heights. Australia had been blooded. Australia had been tried and not found wanting. All the world looked up to the effortless mighty endeavour and contempt for all odds displayed by the Anzac soldiers at the Dardanelles. Further to mark the day, men of the newly-raised and all-Tasmanian 40th battalion marched to a reception equally as emotional as that offered to the 12th—which had covered itself with glory at Gallipoli, and included many Tasmanians in its ranks.

When Hughes decided to put the case for conscription to the people at a plebiscite in 1916, being unable to get legislation through the Labor-dominated Senate, he set fire to a fuse which blew the Labor party to smithereens. In Tasmania, Earle had first of all opposed conscription but after conferring with Hughes in Melbourne, he changed his mind.

This *volte-face* had the effect of confirming the trade union movement's worst suspicions about their leader and his attachment to the ideals of the party. Earle's actions also had the effect of bringing the industrial and parliamentary wings of the movement together when it appeared a split was possible.

Conscription meetings were marked with violence, frequently

The 40th Battalion, AIF, 1916

caused by men in uniform attacking anti-conscriptionists. Censorship prevented full reports from being published, though the *Daily Post* was one of the few, if not the only, daily in the nation to hammer the conscriptionists. Such purveyors of news as the *Mercury* filled the role of dutiful propaganda sheets for those who wanted conscription and opposed Labor.

Frank Anstey made guest appearances and created great uproar when he continued to allege that Hughes had made a deal to import foreign labour if conscription was approved. Hughes himself attracted huge crowds for his memorable performances, simplifying the case to one in which all who dared to vote against conscription were traitors or worse. The highly emotional state of the people was exacerbated by the constant casualty lists from France and the suggestion from such as the *Mercury* that German money was being used to help the anti-conscriptionsts. Not least, no Irish Catholic leader strongly opposed conscription in Tasmania and indeed the eloquent and flamboyant Father T. J. O'Donnell very actively supported it. When a bomb was exploded at a conscription meeting at Beaconsfield in October, it was stated that clearly only an anti-conscriptionist would detonate such a fiendish device though, curiously enough, no one was ever charged with any offence.

In Tasmania as elsewhere the Germans were portrayed in cartoons as unspeakable savages; every useful prejudice was called up and despite Hughes's numerous tactical blunders, such as enrolling men for home service, loyal Tasmania revealed the depth of its feelings by voting strongly in favour of conscription— 49 493 to 37 833. The conscription vote included the strongly Labor west coast, but here the popular hero King O'Malley had remained silent on the issue and Earle, the local boy made good, favoured it, revealing the extent of patriotism in the mining community. It was of great significance, in terms of attitudes to the war, however, that the largely-rural electorate of Franklin came closest to voting 'No'. This lends great strength to the argument that country people feared further labour shortages if conscription were introduced. But the vote was such that indeed the fruitful question is, why did so many vote in favour of conscription?

Joseph Lyons became state parliamentary leader of Labor when Earle resigned and shortly confronted the problems of a general

THE ANTI'S CREED

I believe the men at the Front should be sacrificed.

I believe we should turn dog on them.

I believe that our women should betray the men who are fighting for them.

I believe in the sanctity of my own life.

I believe in taking all the benefit and none of the risks.

I believe it was right to sink the *Lusitania*.

I believe in murder on the high seas.

I believe in the I.W.W.

I believe in Sinn Fein.

I believe that Britain should be crushed and humiliated.

I believe in the massacre of Belgian priests.

I believe in the murder of women, and baby-killing.

I believe that Nurse Cavell got her deserts.

I believe that treachery is a virtue.

I believe that disloyalty is true citizenship.

I believe that desertion is ennobling.

I believe in Considine, Fihelly, Ryan, Blackburn, Brookfield, Mannix, and all their works.

I believe in egg power rather than man power.

I believe in holding up transports and hospital ships.

I believe in general strikes.

I believe in burning Australian haystacks.

I believe in mine-laying in Australian waters.

I believe in handing Australia over to Germany.

I believe I'm worm enough to vote No.

Those who DON'T Believe in the above Creed

will VOTE YES

Authorised by the Reinforcements Referendum Council.   CLAUDE McKAY, Publicity Secretary, 308 Collins Street, Melbourne.

No. 27.   D. W. PATERSON Co. PTY. LTD , Printers, 495 Collins Street, Melbourne.

The upheaval of conscription, 1917

election when Hughes's Labor defectors plus the Liberals combined to inflict a crushing defeat on Labor in 1917; the party so recently in office in Tasmania won no seats in any of the Tasmanian electorates for the House of Representatives and no seats in the Senate. Even the crafty King O'Malley was defeated, but his opponent did drop dead only five days afterwards; he was succeeded by W. G. Spence, the great trade union organizer of yesteryear, though the Tasmanians were loath to vote for an absentee and ex-Labor man. Successive by-elections confirmed the triumph of the anti-Labor forces in 1917, and the crushing of the General Strike that same year by hunger and employment of 'loyalists' brought Labor to the lowest ebb ever in its short history in the island state.

The situation in Russia and the slaughter on the Western Front in 1917 induced Hughes to try again for conscription, but he lost allies by suddenly closing the electoral rolls as if afraid to permit the people to enrol, disfranchising people of German origin and changing polling day from a Saturday to a Thursday for the first time ever. People became more suspicious of Hughes's authoritarian proclivities. The 'No' vote in Tasmania was directed by a youthful Labor man named Robert Cosgrove and much made of the treatment dished out to conscientious objectors in New Zealand, where conscription had been adopted. Tasmanians rather tended to look to New Zealand, as fellow islanders, as fellow high-loyalists and as a people who could teach Tasmanians a few tricks about farming.

The campaign this time was marked by the *Mercury's* tirade against Catholics, helped along by the Easter Rising of 1916 and encouraged by the suspicion of isolated Protestant Tasmanians of a religious group which worshipped in a foreign language and therefore could not possibly be true-blue despite the sudden enlistment in the AIF of Father O'Donnell, after an emotional speaking campaign in favour of conscription. The mood was changing though: now increasing numbers of returned soldiers actually went on to the platform to denounce conscription. Women became more active in the campaign, and when the day of voting came on 20 December, Tasmania voted 38 881 in favour and 38 502 against. This was amazing, for some 10 000 people who voted in 1916 had not voted in 1917 at all, revealing reservations about Hughes, and a majority of more than 10 000 shrunk to 379.

Father O'Donnell, 'abbé and squire' of the north-west coast, 1926

There were those observers who saw the hand of the *Daily Post* and Dwyer-Gray in this result, for the arguments from that quarter had been dignified and reasonable throughout, in marked contrast to the eldritch screeches of other newspapers. Again the central and south rural areas of the state tended to vote against conscription more than some would have judged from their political flavour. The west coast swung back towards the 'No' position.

The war appeared likely to go on forever. By the end of 1917, Tasmania had enlisted 14 205 men. New sectarianism emerged as patriots sought for a scapegoat, and a Loyalty League was formed to root out undesirables, first in Launceston. It flourished especially along the north-west coast where there was a very high percentage of Methodists, perhaps the highest in Australia. They were especially distrustful of Catholics perhaps because Wesley's undemonstrative religious services, as they had developed by the early twentieth century, found Roman ritual particularly offensive and unpalatable. More than that, however, it was the loyalty of distant and vulnerable Tasmania to the Empire that sharpened the sense of threat, real or imagined, from the Catholics, the age-old enemy of Protestant England—and Catholic was identified with Ireland, that springboard from which the Old Country's enemies on continental Europe had ever sought to launch themselves on Protestant England. Every schoolchild in Tasmania knew the stirring story of Good Queen Elizabeth, Sir Francis Drake and the defeat of Catholic Spain.

With the ending of the war, anti-German feeling burst out again even in victory—especially in victory—with the demand for punitive indemnities from Germany, held to be true cause of all the misery and the deaths of so many Tasmanian boys. There was a fight in the lobby of parliament between H. J. Payne and G. C. Becker, the former sneering at the latter as 'Herr' Becker. Tasmanians of German origin suffered silently, and continued to do so all their lives.

The survivors and heroes of the glorious AIF began to arrive home to hysterical welcomes from the people and very slow administration by the Repatriation Department (which should properly have been named the Rehabilitation Department). Unemployment increased and the Returned Soldiers' and Sailors' Imperial League of Australia, knowing the physical and moral strength it mustered, left no doubt it would fight for soldiers' rights of employment. By October 1919 it had 7000 members, some of whom terrorized Labor speakers to such an extent that Launceston City Council refused permission for open-air political meetings. Loyalty to England and the Empire was never so high and implacable opposition never so great towards anyone who thought the war not right and spoke in favour of anything un-British.

In this paranoid atmosphere the Loyalty League flourished as it extended its perception of the threat of Catholicism and Sinn Fein to the threat of everything and anything which was thought currently or at some time in the future to threaten the Anglo-Saxon Protestant ideal.

In 1919 Labor was defeated shatteringly and appeared to be down for the count, because in seeking to win back its erstwhile supporters, the party stranded itself between Left and Right and appeared nothing to everybody. In these dark days of defeat, Labor's first premier John Earle found it within his saddened soul to liken his former party mates to whipped curs howling in the night. The Great War had accomplished some terrible things.

One thing the Great War did was to create an elite of returned men in the society, their quality of heroism emphasized every Anzac Day, their superior manliness and status exemplified by soldier preference in employment. But for most people the immediate effect of the war was the most obvious one: about 13 000 sons of the state embarked for the war and nearly 2500 were killed. The losses the people were called upon to bear were never to be forgotten. On many a plain living-room wall there had appeared the strange dignity of stiff photographs of men in uniform who, it was stated in writing, had fought for God, King and Country—and who did not come back to the plains and bush, the paddocks and the streets of their beloved island. Men who had never handled anything but an axe had learnt to handle a rifle, and did not return. Those who did survive were frequently never the same men again: some became drunkards, some became steady and swore the Great War was the best thing that ever happened to them; some knocked their wives about and committed terrible crimes; some returned to their employment as if nothing had happened to them and thought little of medals and glowing testimonials in Bean's *Official History of Australia in the Great War*;

some who had gone into the Somme at the age of sixteen and seen and done things they could not begin to imagine, returned to a shiftless life and, like so many others, migrated inter-state and joined the 6th Division in 1939.

On King Island there had been a population of 1000 people, and 63 men enlisted and 8 were killed; from Ulverstone's total population of 2000, 243 men joined the AIF and 55 were killed; at the nearby township of Penguin, 107 men enlisted from a population of 1120, and 26 did not return; from the mining centre of Queenstown, 300 men enlisted from a total population of 3700 and 55 were killed. Somewhere between one third and one-half of all eligible males in Tasmania enlisted in the AIF.

Far from home had the heroes been slain. The gratification of a family funeral, so important in that era, was denied their next of kin so that Anzac Day became a time of annual mass obsequies to compensate, the service conducted at the closed grave of the local war memorial. Perhaps there was a sinking feeling that the boys of Tasmania perished and fought for less than worthy objects . . . but that was an unthinkable thought and the Anzac legend and tradition was firmly fixed in place as a sort of defence mechanism. No relatives had gazed on the face of the fallen, as had the kings and clan chiefs of their distant forebears so that those responsible might ponder on their conduct in causing such death and pain. Few if any Tasmanian next of kin would ever manage the journey to the other side of the world to see the the grave of the soldier. There remained in the memory of many grieving Tasmanians only the sounds of the distant marching, only the shouts of a vanished army.

6

Distress

When the Earle Labor government was defeated in 1916, Walter Lee became premier. As elsewhere in Australia, the Labor party was disheartened by what appeared to be the collapse of reason among the working classes of the world who had not paused to join the rival armies in what some Labor men believed to be a trade conflict in which the working class would fight, bleed and die for the increasing profits of arms manufacturers and others who would do well out of the war. In Tasmania the party was also downcast thanks to the upheaval of the 1916 conscription plebiscite and the Australia-wide destruction it had wrought among Labor supporters, not least being the apostasy of Earle.

In 1919 Lee's Nationalists, as they were now christened, won the state election, the same year as the men of the AIF began returning and the island was smitten by the Spanish influenza pandemic. Fortunately this struck the island late in the winter when people's resistance was improving; the dispersed character of the population of Tasmania also evidently made the spread of the infection more difficult for the deadly virus. Many efforts were made to prevent the flu, including sealing off the island insofar as was possible and greatly inconveniencing tourists, imposing quarantine, and using cotton masks which were about as useful as using barbed-wire fences to keep out mosquitoes. Medical science did not know what to do about the flu and the disease created great alarm in Tasmania as elsewhere in Australia.

The government was concerned about the outbreak and deaths and signs of panic: the face of the victim was apt to become discoloured, and the horrifying ghost of Black Death walked again among the more credulous. An emergency committee was appointed and all Hobart divided into thirteen districts, each supervised by a clergyman who visited every dwelling to report on the needs of those suffering from the flu. But this led to an unexpected finding because the visitors seeking to succour the victims of the pandemic found evidence of living conditions so appalling as to be unbelievable.

So alarmed was the Rev. H. E. Hobday that he persuaded a reporter from the *Mercury* to accompany him on his rounds and there was published a series of articles which shocked the respectable. 'In Darkest Hobart' was the title of the stories, printed in September 1919. Therein were described hovels worse than any in the East End of London where rents were high and ceilings low, families large and rooms small, the floors eaten by rats and walls swarming with bugs.

Several of these disgraceful dwellings were discovered to be owned by those described delicately as 'public men'. Such a place in Argyle Street consisted of one room divided into three, with no fireplace except in the tiny kitchen. In the centre 'room' a married couple and their five children were all recovering from three weeks' illness caused by the flu. The investigators found widespread unemployment and under-nourishment beneath their very noses. In parliament the radical David Dicker, who had been persecuted during the war because two visiting actresses said they heard him say something which might prejudice recruiting, observed that wealthy men in Hobart were now taking action to clean up sources of ill-health because they were afraid they too might fall victim to the flu.

Certainly a Home bill to make provision for the construction of houses and advances of loans for approved building was passed as investigators stressed the necessity for reform, but as the crisis subsided few fundamental changes were made.

The return of the first members of the AIF to be discharged led to what became known as the soldier settlement scheme. Early in 1916 a national meeting in Melbourne decided with enthusiasm that returned heroes should be settled on the land, a step in line with pre-war concern about closer settlement and reduction of large estates. In November the Lee government introduced such legislation. Some members of parliament who knew the difficulties of farming and whose judgement was not clouded by feverish patriotism, were doubtful about such a plan but pride in the AIF, continued recruiting drives which necessarily elevated the volunteer soldier as a hero, and the premier's natural impatience all combined to encourage the idea. An impulse as least as ancient as Alexander's and Caesar's settlement of their demobilized warriors on the land emerged in the form of a statement that any Tasmanian who returned from the front line would be given free a piece of the precious island he had been fighting to defend from the Kaiser's ambition. The fantasy of the sturdy yeoman and the idyll of the good life to be enjoyed only in communion with nature and her bounty, was flourishing like the green bay tree.

The basic ideology of the scheme was not the only thing wrong. Selection of applications was defective as well as the allocation of blocks and finance. Incredibly for a state in which the agricultural land had been made fruitful only by incredible toil and hardship, the Lee administration arranged no preliminary training programme for the potential farmer. This became part of the impossible duties of the inspectors attached to the closer settlement board who travelled tremendous distances each year seeking to help the hapless soldier-settler.

In the first year after peace, the board calculated that perhaps half the new men were making good progress but that nearly one in five was making none at all. The board solemnly declared, against all the evidence of practical observers, that want of knowledge, thrift and perseverance was the trouble. There were other problems. Some men were rendered unfit for farming as the result of physical or mental war wounds. Some soldier-settlers reacted to the peaceful environment of their home island by seeking sudden and violent change and then equally as impulsively craved complete rest. In 1926 it was stated that too many men drank, destroyed their properties and were dishonest, and that they had indeed been advised by members of parliament not to pay their instalments.

To meet its undertaking, the government also purchased going concerns and this of course led to increased prices all round and raised rents. The result was that repayments could not always be met and the board continued to receive heart-breaking, angry, or bitter and bewildered letters from ex-soldiers begging to have their repayments decreased or waived until they got a start.

Land was also subdivided along the earlier lines of closer settlement but on no clear economic principle: the average size of the farms in the Richmond district was a little over forty acres, and in the Oatlands and Penguin areas, down to twenty-five acres.

Some such properties, if carefully and skilfully managed, could be made to pay but bad seasons and low prices, together with increased freight costs, told against even the best or most fortunate soldier-settler.

By the mid-1920s the rural idyll had, yet again in the history of Australia, been revealed to be rubbish in the majority of cases. Ten years after the end of the conflict in Europe, only about 800 of 2000 soldier-settlers survived on their farms in Tasmania. Under-capitalization, the depredations of rabbits, the ruin of the Irish blight in potato-growing areas, and the lack of skill on the part of the ex-soldiers, all put paid to the dream of many a settler.

In June 1926 the government in time-honoured style appointed a Royal Commission to investigate the disaster; the board and various interested parties contrived to keep the sad facts a secret, though experienced farmers who lived near soldier-settlers were only too aware of their problems. It was the crowning irony of the entire farcical business that the commissioner appointed knew little of farming. Such was one result of the men of the state answering the call to defend the British Empire and its values as they appeared in Tasmania.

In 1922 the Lee Nationalist government won the state election again but there was turmoil in parliament. Post-war prosperity was not evident in Tasmania. A newly-formed Country party emerged and the Labor party revived with men such as J. Lyons and, above all, A. G. Ogilvie making themselves prominent, as the harassed Lee administration appeared unable to meet the expectations of the people after the war to end all war. Still, wages boards had been reconstituted in 1920 but the Nationalist party declined as it became clear that the finances of the state were not in good order. Workers' Educational Association work was suspended and even school dental clinics closed in 1923 as economy measures. As the Nationalists became more dissatisfied with their leadership, so did Labor under Lyons become more confident and strike a note of authority. A group of turbulent government members voting with Lyons, the Lee government collapsed, there was a brief interlude under the leadership of J. B. Hayes and then in October 1923, Lyons became premier. A vote of no confidence in the new government was lost when no fewer than seven Nationalists and their allies voted for Labor.

Labor may have been in office in the House of Assembly but

A. G. Ogilvie, Labor premier of Tasmania 1934–9

it was certainly not in power, because it was confronted with the Legislative Council, a body which continued to oppose progressive legislation in season and out.

In 1922 and 1923 it had emasculated Lee's financial policy in its desire for greater economy; its opposition to what it termed 'labour legislation' assisted the Nationalists to their demise in 1923. The advent of a Labor administration naturally offended the Council and confirmed its unswerving opposition to parliamentary democracy based on one value, one vote. Clearly here was an unequivocal sign that the pretensions of the people required to be crushed and their daring conduct reduced to its natural deference and timidity. The Council's ideological position translated in practical terms to a belief that financial difficulties could be resolved by sacking public servants and, where that was impossible, reducing their salaries.

In the three years following Labor's victory, proposed legislation rejected by the Council included a Workers' Compensation Act Amendment Bill, an Occupational Diseases Bill, a State Arbitration Court Bill, a Fair Rents Bill and a Rating Reform Bill. Even when employers and employees agreed on moderate and useful legislation, the Council destroyed it. It is a remarkable fact that even the *Mercury* began to grow uneasy when the Council insulted the intelligence of the House of Assembly by rejecting the Arbitration Bill: was it possible that the Council might actually cause irresistible pressure for its reform or abolition?

In 1924 it appeared that the Council had gone too far when it amended a money bill which the Assembly claimed was equivalent to delaying the voting of Supply, and thus endangered the ordinary service of government to the public. But what were the legal powers of the Council? No one really knew. The chief executive of the day was the Administrator, Sir Herbert Nicholls, a new governor being awaited. Nicholls agreed to sign the bill as it left the Assembly, and at Lyons's request, simply disregarded the Council. That body of course was most put out and upset, representing as it thought the best interests of the state. In these circumstances, the government sought the advice of London whereat the Secretary of State advised the Administrator to ask the law officers of the government what they thought. These officers advised Nicholls to keep on signing. He did and an instructive encounter shaped itself.

Even the people had a say, because following the government's persistence in ignoring the Council, a state election was held, and won by Labor. This was a most inconvenient result for the Council and consultations between it and the House commenced. As a result of meetings between J. Lyons, A. G. Ogilvie and R. Cosgrove (for the government), and F. B. Edwards, T. Shields and C. Eady (for the Council) a decision was reached which embodied agreement that the Council had the power to reject money bills. An impression of the people's sovereignty was conveyed by a further agreement that the Council could only suggest amendments for certain other financial proposals which, however, were to be on an annual basis.

If anything could be concluded from these transactions, it was that the Council emerged with its powers virtually unimpaired. Credit or otherwise for this was attributed to F. B. Edwards and H. B. White, the latter the parliamentary draftsman. It is interesting that Labor's policy was in fact abolition of the Council.

Prior to his succession to power, Lyons had made numerous powerful attacks on the evils of capitalism and the prospects of war and misery said to be carried within it, but during his premiership, little more than lip-service was paid to such ideology. It is highly significant that his wife (later to become Dame Enid Lyons) induced this Labor premier to cancel his subscription to the *Australian Worker* because the official Labor publication, she judged, was too biased, intolerant and bitter.

Other factors watered down Lyons' radicalism, not least of which was his increasing preoccupation with Tasmania's economic difficulties under federation. It was a crowning irony that the customs union sought for so long by Tasmania should turn out to be judged by the people as an absolute curse. During Lyons's term of office, and before, publicists unwearyingly drew attention to the high taxes paid in Tasmania, and to the adverse effects of the Navigation Act, the provisions of which were brought into operation in March 1920.

This was a constant source of complaint in Tasmania because it was held to lead to increased freight charges and leave the island more and more at the mercy of the shipping lines. The principal plaint was that ship-owners, under the act, were obliged to pay wages and maintain conditions which led to high charges, avoidable if wholesome competition were permitted. It was said that the tourist trade suffered as well and that overseas vessels could not carry inter-state passengers unless the ships complied with the provisions of the act.

Worst of all, a series of maritime strikes dislocated shipping services and left Tasmania without the important tourist trade in summer. In successive seasons there was a coal strike, the Spanish flu and a seamen's strike. It was all too much. The *Mercury* summed up the feelings of many Tasmanians, especially those in the south (including the jam magnate Sir Henry Jones) when it condemned the Navigation Act, the arbitration system, and Australia's tariff policy as a triple-headed vampire which sucked Tasmania white.

Since the Tasmanian Grant Act of 1912, disability payments had been made by the Commonwealth to a total of £500 000 over ten years. That arrangement expired in 1921 but was continued till some permanent scheme could be devised, and this turned out to be the Tasmanian Sinking Fund Agreement of 1928. A Royal Commission found that Tasmania's difficulties would not be materially decreased by sweeping away the Navigation Act. Amendments to it did permit the carriage of passengers between Tasmania and the mainland, but the overseas shipping companies did not take advantage of this. The expected benefits from federation were proving to be an empty dream and Tasmania discovered that companies did not invest as an act of social policy.

In 1925 a Tasmanian Rights League was formed, to be representative of all localities and political opinions, in response to what was perceived as the failure of the Bruce–Page federal government to recognize Tasmania's claims. It sought a federal ferry service with ships manned by employees of the federal authority. The *Mercury* agitated for secession, Launceston wanted ships run by non-union labour.

Beset with difficulties as he was, Lyons stressed more and more the non-party conduct of government; he spoke of the interests of all Tasmanians; he disarmed the Opposition by his patent sincerity and willingness to run what was really an informal coalition ministry; he came to see militant industrial action as unpalatable, and perceived the strike weapon solely as action by one part of the community against another. Lyons appointed Sir James O'Grady, a former British Trades Union Congress president, as governor of the state. This underlined the premier's patriotism and classless attitude at a time when similar views were held by the powerful RSSILA; no one was as loyal to the Crown and Empire as J. A. Lyons (Catholic and anti-conscriptionist); the Duke of York nowhere received a more loyal welcome than in Tasmania when he came to open the federal parliament at Canberra in 1927.

Yet in 1928, at the state election, Lyons was still automatically opposed by the Tasmanian press which decided that all the good he was said to have done was really due to the Nationalist Opposition, led by J. C. McPhee. Confronted with this perfidy, the premier thanked the press for playing the game. In many ways Lyons succeeded, where S. M. Bruce failed, in de-politicizing politics in the period after the Great War. He did it by neglecting to pursue Labor policies even when the finances of Tasmania, thanks to federal subventions in large part, had become less shaky, and when he had an elected majority in the House of Assembly. No doubt the existence of the Council would have prevented much or indeed any progressive legislation from being passed without considerable difficulty, but Lyons failed to reveal to the people how the Council treated the people's representatives. Even moderate Labor supporters found the Premier's conduct increasingly hard to swallow.

Worse than that was the Lyons government's reduction of land and income tax, against ALP policy, in such a way that the middle and small landholder was seen to be shabbily treated. The final difficulty of Lyons's position was revealed when this legislation was attacked by the Nationalists on behalf of the small property owners and working classes. Lyons would have made—perhaps indeed was—an excellent Nationalist. He resisted the Hobart Trades Hall Council in an attempt before election to obtain from all Labor candidates an undertaking that there would not be any deviation from Labor policy and that there should be legislation passed in accordance with that policy. The THC was especially unhappy at the Lyons government's refusal to put up a bill giving preference to trade unionists and establishing a 44-hour week.

Lyons was defeated in 1928 when representation fell in the south. The worsening economic plight of the state, with the approach of the Depression, was one reason; J. C. McPhee's capable leadership of the Nationalists was another. There was also Lyons's failure since 1927 to have a southern representative in his ministry, there was a scandal concerning Ogilvie and his legal firm's connections with a trust fund, there was a fear indeed that the active Ogilvie himself would succeed Lyons, and there was the failure of Lyons to re-admit G. W. Mahoney to the party after he stood as an Independent Labor candidate.

At this defeat, perhaps the premier had begun to realize that he had been too easy-going and trusting and all things to all men. The out-going leader of the ALP expressed sorrow and disappointment that his political opponents had not played the game when they boasted that the Opposition should take any credit going. Lyons had pleased many Tasmanians but disappointed the generation which perceived in the triumph of Lenin and the Bolsheviks a harbinger of social justice and prosperity for all, and that indeed the meek would inherit the earth.

J. C. McPhee succeeded Lyons in June 1928 on the eve of the Great Depression. He became interested in public affairs as a result of his activities in the Australian Natives' Association and the temperance movement. His administration was confronted with the intractable problems of the Depression and unemployment, and obliged to preside over a period when the Premiers' Plan adopted conventional economic wisdom and reduced public expenditure till something should turn up. Record floods in 1929 added to the increasing misery of the people when Launceston and the north in general suffered from an extraordinary rainfall.

Such was the onslaught of the Depression that the people affected were scarcely able to consider the source of it, though to many who had been out of work in the 1920s anyway, the Depression represented little in the way of change. In 1928, unemployment among reporting trade unions was about 11 per cent but leapt to 27 per cent in 1931 and 26 per cent in 1932, before dropping slowly to 7–8 per cent in the two years before the war of 1939–45.

What was to be done about the huge number of unemployed? With a distinct prospect of turbulent spirits asking questions about the causes of social upheaval and hardships in the land of the working man's paradise, the McPhee government sought to integrate unemployment relief policies and the rural sector. This was partly because the constraints of wages boards and arbitration awards would thus be avoided and primary production increased with the aid of the Department of Agriculture. With some caution, Ogilvie agreed to co-operate in this great emergency, though suspicious that the plan would be used by some to grease the fat sow, as he put it.

Subsidies were offered to property-owners in this business-led recovery scheme, leading to criticism that interest-free loans were going the way of the rich, and that women were employing their husbands. In 1932, Lyons as Prime Minister now became more involved in relief schemes when state and federal authorities contributed to a fund whereby the municipalities were enabled to borrow at low interest, the scheme to be administered by the state unemployment councils. In addition money was granted in the form of unemployment allowances to prospectors, with aid for experimental rock-drilling and boring operations in the industry.

McPhee's government survived the election of 1931, a measure of the Opposition's policy because Ogilvie established links with J. T. Lang, the fiery premier of New South Wales. It did not go down well in loyal and patriotic Tasmania when the leader of the state Labor party declared that the breakdown of the monetary system was the cause of unemployment. Ogilvie also did not gain votes by drawing attention to the pitiful exhibition of Lyons and the state premiers down on their knees begging the Commonwealth Bank Board and its chairman, Sir Robert Gibson, for some tokens with which to trade. Ogilvie continued to condemn the policy recommended by Sir Otto Niemeyer, the visiting agent of the British banks, because, said Ogilvie, those people who continued to draw interest were increasing purchasing power at the expense of the workers.

Echoing Lang, the Labor party in Tasmania sought postponement of the payment of overseas interest till the government and the British bond-holders agreed to an equitable reduction in interest and a just scheme for the liquidation of capital liabilities. Advising the federal government was ironically enough a son of Tasmania—L. F. Giblin, gallant officer in the 40th Battalion, a member of the Tasmanian Labor party and one who had shared a study at Cambridge with J. M. Keynes. This experience did not notably make him a Keynesian.

Probably the major undertaking or private project in Tasmania for the relief of unemployment was the YMCA occupational scheme. Established first in Hobart in the second half of 1931, and then at Launceston and on the north-west coast, it sought to train

L. F. Giblin (1872–1951), soldier and economist

boys aged between fourteen and twenty for agricultural work and for employment in industrial trades and clerical pursuits. One of the impulses was a fear of demoralization and anarchy among the unemployed and the danger of the future adults of the state becoming wasters.

In this scheme, farms, or 'colonies', were purchased by the government to train youths in forestry and agriculture. Farmers stood ready to accept boys, despite Labor protests that it was an example of sweating and a disgrace that these boys were to be paid only 5s. a week to work for farmers for nothing.

In addition, a Toc H mothers' and girls' club was set up to train girls for service and to make clothes for distribution among the unemployed. Girls' classes were established and, to avoid compromising morals, lounges for the unmarried were opened each evening, where there was community singing, games, and talks of an uplifting character.

Church of England men's societies also conducted an unemployment scheme in Hobart to find odd jobs. Here the

Mercury and wireless station 7ZL publicized the idea to purchase small plots of land whereon the unemployed might grow vegetables . . . but there was a problem in this because such Christian charity led to competition with other gardeners. Rotarians also made an effort to help their fellow-Tasmanians in a 'spend for unemployment' campaign on a state-wide basis, in the belief that expansion of private credit was the most appropriate measure to revive the economy.

Returned soldiers were also active, demanding a reasonable share of preference in distribution of relief work. Lee refused and informed the RSSILA that his chief concern was provision for the most necessitous cases as they arose. There emerged an Anzac Relief Association, its exertions lent point by the most strong objections to the idea of repudiation of overseas debts, as suggested by such as J. T. Lang. RSSILA spokesmen contrasted the traitorous proposal of repudiation with the honour, self-respect and reputation of the Empire and themselves as guardians and custodians of the memories of the Great War. That was in August 1932, and the RSSILA introduced a civil patrol movement, supported by voluntary public subscriptions and supervised by the police, to provide householders with such services as protection of their homes. Some saw this as an excellent precaution to safe-guard the property of the people when repudiationists stalked the land, others saw it as the preliminary move to establishment of a fascist New Guard.

But the typical response to the Depression in Tasmania was the self-help scheme. Such a one was conducted by the young men of St Andrew's Church, Launceston. Here were made toy aero-planes, wheelbarrows, hobby horses and folding chairs. The community assisted by donating cases and other such raw materials.

There were always trouble-makers, however, complained the do-gooders, and considerable disquiet arose when communists gained influential positions in the Unemployed Workers' Movement. Particularly was this so in Launceston, and it drew a predictable reaction from the city council and ex-servicemen. In Hobart, however, moderates such as G. W. Mahoney gained control of the UWM and at Glenorchy they were openly antagonistic to communists. At the Beaconsfield Forestry Reserve, however, a government announcement that wages would be reduced from 12s. to 10s. a day led to a disturbing series of incidents, involving the UWM threatening to intimidate scab workers. There was a demonstration in Launceston but the UWM was compelled to back down.

The UWM was also very suspicious of the government's establishment of 'concentration' camps of single men, which it was feared would be conducted by the military and used to break strikes. There were confrontations, moreover, between members of the UWM and returned soldiers. On Anzac Day 1931 in Launceston the display of red flags infuriated the loyalists, who burnt them, together with a large calico notice outside a house, stating that the occupant had served in the war 1915–18 with the result that he now had no work, no home and no rent. Loyalists publicly threatened decisive action against those judged less than true to God, King and country, and of a low standard of morality. For its part, the Launceston city council cracked down on those it considered were disloyal, despite objections to the ban raised by three of its alderman, the ALP, the WEA and the Freedom of Speech League. The anti-British tone of the radicals and communists—or, rather, their conviction that there were higher and more worthy objects than mindless adulation of the Empire—was particularly offensive in loyal Tasmania.

When a reinvigorated Labor party won office in 1934, and no fewer than thirteen new members were elected, the worst of the Depression was over but the distribution of relief remained one of the principal duties of government. The confusion of private schemes, charities and government responsibility led to a most rigorous examination of persons seeking relief. In 1934, for instance, applicants could be refused if they possessed a player piano, wireless set, motor, or cart and horse. Persons seeking relief were obliged to register at the Public Works Department in Hobart or Launceston, or at local council chambers, where wardens obtained a police report on the applicant and then decided on the amount of aid to be offered. Orders for provisions depended upon the number of dependants and whether or not the person was in the town or country. The basic rate was 7s. 6d. worth of rations a week, and recipients of the dole were permitted, in addition to sustenance, to earn the value of their rent plus up to 10s. a week for a worker with four or more children. Single unemployed women not living in their parents' home were generally ignored though some sustenance was paid in winter. The need for constant re-application, stern control, a harsh adminis-tration and the social disgrace of applying for relief meant that dole seekers had frequently exhausted all their resources before making application.

With the coming to office of the ALP in 1934, new government enterprises began to absorb a number of the unemployed, in the form of works for the Hydro-Electric Commission, established by a statute of 1929, the Public Works Department, Forestry Department and so on. On taking office, Labor increased sustenance and work for dole rates by 20 per cent in the cities and 30 per cent in the country when it took money from the consoli-dated revenue of the preceding government.

The solution to unemployment in Tasmania lay largely in the hands of the federal government, and certainly the Lyons admin-istration in Canberra did allocate some funds for public works and mining. Municipalities came to handle the matter locally, with

Multiple arch dam, Miena, *c.* 1927

state and federal funds. Thus it was that the road to the top of Mt Wellington ('Ogilvie's scar') was completed, but some local government authorities were slow to use the facility of money offered. Launceston council was one such, and Kingborough council refused with great hilarity a request for a first-aid kit for the men employed on local government relief works. One councillor said that the next thing would be a request for armchairs, and another representative observed that the men were not likely to work hard enough to have an accident. Thus was the Depression lightened and enlivened for some by local government wit.

The principal social problem was in the cities, because farmers tended to employ relatives in unpaid but sustaining work, and the relatively small number of people affected made the problem less difficult for government. The Hobart Relief Canteen feared, as did many, the results of the Depression, because it perceived people with their spirits broken to such an extent that it would be difficult for them ever again to regain former courage and outlook, modest as that might have been. Medical men reported that the standard of health was more a social problem than a medical one: insufficient clothing and under-feeding made the people a prey to disease, and observers continued to worry about what would become of the rising generation, starved and dispirited as some of it now was. An official school nurse reported that one in eight of the children she supervised was suffering from some degree of malnutrition. At Wellington Square school, Launceston, hot milk was distributed daily to more than 170 undernourished children. The Salvation Army soup kitchen in Hobart in the winter of 1938 supplied soup and bread each day to 150 families, including 1500 children; in June 1939, some 200 persons a day were still being succoured in this way.

Though the government did take responsibility for some sustenance, it was reluctant to accept any for housing and clothing. This was a field where charity could do its age-old work, but the government was obliged to provide boots when men began arriving for work on the Mt Wellington road wearing dancing shoes, sandshoes and slippers in 1934, discovering the truth, if they did not already know it, of the old adage, Cold as charity.

The administration of A. G. Ogilvie which took office in 1934, and extended the duration of parliament to five years, became associated in the people's minds with the gradual emergence of the state from the miseries of the Depression. Ogilvie was a lawyer who joined the Labor party and became a member of parliament in 1919. In 1923 he became attorney-general in the Lyons government, was made a King's Counsel in 1925 (the youngest in the Empire) and gained a great reputation for vigorous debate and, unfortunately for him, for shrewdness verging on sharpness . . . but he remained in power till his sudden death in 1939 at the age of forty-seven, after he had won a great victory at the polls with a most able team of ministers including Robert Cosgrove, T. G. D'Alton, E. Dwyer-Gray, J. F. Gaha, T. H. Davies and E. J. Ogilvie.

The Labor government increased the construction programme of the Hydro-Electric Commission and built a new power station at Tarraleah, giving at once a general hope for new industry and immediate hope and income for the victims of the Depression. Newsprint was also promoted as an industry well-suited for an island with Tasmania's timber resources. In 1937, Australian newspaper proprietors amalgamated with Sir Keith Murdoch's Derwent Valley Company Pty Ltd, to form Australian Newsprint Mills Ltd, and in 1937 Ogilvie made available a large concession at the headwaters of the River Derwent, in difficult mountain country. At about the same time at Boyer, near New Norfolk, was established a newsprint mill. With L. R. S. Benjamin as general manager, it became the first enterprise in the world to produce newsprint from hardwood. At Burnie, similar concessions were granted to Associated Pulp and Paper Mills and hydro power made available.

In the early part of the century, a Department of Public Health was established in Tasmania, under Dr J. S. C. Elkington who led the fight against smallpox, and exhorted local authorities to look to the health of the community. His greatest work was in recording the health of children, and books he wrote on it became models of their kind. By 1911 Elkington and his department had reduced infant mortality from 111 per 1000 to 76. Under successive managements, by 1917 the child welfare scheme had accomplished a further decrease to 21 deaths per 1000 births. Investigation of goitre was commenced in 1921 and Ogilvie's government brought in free medical services to rural areas and did a great deal in the improvement of health. New hospitals were

Burnie Paper Mills, *c.* 1939

built at Hobart and Launceston, the former ironically enough continuing on the site on the banks of that Hobart Town Rivulet which had served as an open sewer and source of disease since Governor Collins's camp in 1804.

From being backward in education, Tasmania from the time of Neale's reforms and his new education in 1905, became very experimental in this field. In the 1920s it achieved three notable firsts when, in the area of infant education, Miss Amy Rowntree launched the first pre-school centres, when a correspondence school was started by R. Solomon in 1919 to help children in isolated areas, and when H. Parker launched Australia's first Department of Educational Psychology section.

During Ogilvie's regime, he began considering the use of wireless for state school education as early as 1925 and a year later proposed swimming instruction. More experiments went forward with the establishment of two area schools at Sheffield and Hagley, to the great interest of educationists elsewhere, to meet the needs of pupils in districts where primary production was dominant.

At the same time the principal private schools continued to

attract pupils, the extension and strengthening of the Catholic schools especially demanding enormous work and sacrifice in the face of the money spent on the state system. St Virgil's College, Hobart, was established in 1911 by the Order of Christian Brothers, St Patrick's in Launceston was also founded by that Order, and the Deloraine Convent started in 1895. St Mary's College, Hobart, was started in 1895 by the Presentation Order of Sisters.

An unusual school was the Society of Friends' School in Hobart, established in 1887 in relationship with a long-standing connection of the colony and state with the Society of Friends. In the north, Scotch College was founded in 1900 and, privately owned, officially recognized by the Presbyterian Churches in 1925. Methodist Ladies' College, Launceston, was established in 1886 and the Collegiate School, Hobart, ten years later. Fahan School for Girls at Sandy Bay came into existence in 1935.

Thus, with the addition of the earlier schools such as Hutchins and Launceston Grammar, Tasmania had a wide variety of schools by the 1930s. Yet for various reasons, the state high schools continued to be held in very high regard by parents, partly due to a succession of resourceful and energetic Ministers and Directors of Education, and because governments came to place public money into the schools which the children of the people were obliged by law to attend. This was also one area where the constraints of travel actually militated in Tasmania's favour. In comparison with other states, the overwhelming majority of the children did not have far to go to school though the terrain might be difficult, and hence the state saved, relatively, on costs of school transport.

As elsewhere in Australia, the 1920s was the age of the 'flapper' and of a new attitude to women. In 1922 two women stood for parliament and a Tasmanian Women's Non-party Political League was formed. The object was to put forward women candidates, to obtain full civil rights for women, to improve conditions in education and public health, to obtain a firmer consideration of social questions and immediately to bring into force the Mental Deficiency Act. The same year Miss B. M. Reed became the first woman dentist in Tasmania, her surgery at Latrobe, in 1923 Launceston's first woman's club was formed, and by 1924 there were women Justices of the Peace.

The movies also caught on in Tasmania as elsewhere, the state getting a bonus in terms of its dual identities as historic and scenic by the appearance of 'For the Term of His Natural Life' on the one hand and 'Jewelled Nights' on the other, the first a lavish film based on Marcus Clarke's famous work, the second a romance adapted from Marie Bjelke-Petersen's novel set in the bush of the north-west coast.

But modernity could be taken too far. In 1926 Ulverstone council forbade the dancing of the Charleston within the municipality and was asked by ministers of religion to close down an open-air palais de danse in the interests of morality. Tasmanian Bright Young Things were checked.

As the government railways continued to lose money, in 1932 the Lyell Highway finally gave the capital of Tasmania a direct road link with the west coast, though there still remaind mining fields which were accessible only by rail, so that local schoolteachers were warned of the approach of department inspectors by a pre-arranged series of whistle-blasts from the engine-driver. The automobile became very popular as elsewhere, leading to construction of new and better roads and expansion of settlement. The Tasmanian Autocar Club was formed by 1911, with a daily motor service running between Burnie and Launceston by 1923. In 1926, to help deal with speeding motorists, all Tasmanian traffic police were trained to estimate speeds, and experiments revealed they were correct about 75 per cent of the time.

From its European settlement, Tasmania depended utterly on sea transport and hence it was not surprising that entrepreneurs should arise in this field very early. The most important in the period between the wars was the Holyman family. In 1919 died William Holyman, father of Thomas Henry, William and James, who became very active in a shipping business, centred at Launceston after moving from Devonport in 1899. By 1931 there were no fewer than nine Holyman steamers playing Australian coastal waters and the company began buying up Bass Strait islands.

Air transport began in Tasmania in 1919 when Lieutenant Arthur Long, of the Australian Flying Corps, flew copies of the *Mercury* from Hobart to Launceston and Deloraine, the first commercial flight in Australia. In December of that year he also made a flight from Stanley to Torquay, Victoria, the first Bass

Strait crossing. Upon his return from the Great War, Victor Holyman established a branch of the Australian Aero Club at Launceston in 1928, and four years later persuaded his family to buy a plane and begin an aerial service between Launceston and Flinders Island. Holyman then joined forces with L. M. Johnson, also on the Flinders Island run, to form Tasmanian Aerial Services Pty Ltd, the necessity for travelling to Bass Strait islands being one of the main impulses which led the Tasmanians to be early aviators.

In 1933 there was completed the first journey to Melbourne via Flinders Island, made by Holyman and Johnson in three and a half hours. When Johnson retired, his interest was purchased by the Holymans, and Holyman Airways Pty Ltd created. As a result of a contract with the federal government, a thrice-weekly air service to Melbourne began in October 1934, but was followed by two fatal crashes in two years. Ten passengers and Vic Holyman were

Sir Ivan Holyman (1896–1957), co-founder of Australian National Airways Pty Ltd killed in one of these. Victor's brother Ivan, however, kept the company intact and in 1936 it amalgamated with Adelaide Airways to form Australian National Airways Pty Ltd, which then branched out to cover all Australia by 1942, and ultimately be absorbed into Ansett Transport Industries Ltd.

Great hopes were held out for the development of Tasmania by the establishment of hydro-electric enterprises and the linking of all centres to this source of energy. Following the takeover in 1916 of a private company experiencing difficulties, two 5000 horse-power turbo-generators were installed at Waddamana to generate power for domestic lighting and trams in Hobart, and three years later a construction programme began for the installation of additional plant at Waddamana. In 1923 Miena Dam at the Great Lake was completed to supply additional power to the Electrolytic Zinc Company and the next year another such dam was constructed at the south end of the lake, blocking the inflow into the River Shannon. Storage capacity was further increased and ultimately the flow directed on to the Waddamana turbines where 63 000 horsepower was generated. Sub-stations reduced the current to a point where general distribution could be accomplished. Rural areas began to receive the boon of electric power and modernization which enabled not only light and electrically-driven pumps and other machinery to be installed, but also electric kitchens, with all their advantages of cleanliness and refrigerated storage of such items as milk. By 1927 a line of electricity had been opened from the Great Lake to Sheffield, Devonport, Ulverstone and Penguin.

The Electrolytic Zinc Company was established during the Great War at Hobart and was headed by H. W. Gepp who, with W. L. Baillieu, set the company on its feet. In a project comparable in scale to the establishment of the Newcastle steel industry, Gepp overcame metallurgical difficulties and in the foundation years designed a plant which came to produce very high quality zinc of 99.95 per cent purity, together with the important by-product, superphosphate. In 1919, the government announced it would spend £2 million on hydro-electricity, and among the beneficiaries was a new enterprise, also at Hobart.

This was Cadbury Brothers' confectionery enterprise at Claremont and in 1920 it obtained an option over 246 acres for a factory. An estate was to be laid out in accordance with modern town-planning principles, along the lines of Bournville in England, and a year later W. Pascall, an English director, arrived to inspect progress.

Other industries started at this time included Kelsall and Kemp Ltd of Rochdale, which opened woollen works in Launceston in 1923; a year later Patons and Baldwins secured 200 acres also at Launceston for a spinning mill.

Those same dairying districts which provided the confectioners Cadbury-Fry-Pascall with milk, frequently also produced potatoes for export to New South Wales. In 1933, as part of the increasingly active intervention of the government, potato seed improvement work began at the Tewkesbury potato research station, south of Burnie, to promote the industry. It was in such areas that victims of the Depression were encouraged to learn agricultural skills.

Water and timber were always abundant in Tasmania and a Forestry Department was formed in 1919 but for some time

Sir H. W. Gepp (1877–1954), general manager of the E. Z. Company received little money. Then in the 1930s the government was informed that past neglect, greed and lack of forestry management had left the state with only fifteen years' supply of timber, and brought action which would at the same time, it was thought, lead to reafforestation, forest management and production of paper pulp.

Associated with Tasmania's natural appearance was the subject of conservation of its resources and exploitation of its environment for the purposes of tourism. In the 1930s little was thought of a serious conflict between these two, but in fact the ground was being laid for a clash of very wide interest. The scenic character of the state and the prospect of tourism had long been realized in Tasmania and the benefit to be derived from visitors acknowledged by the issue in 1899–1900 of Australia's only colonial pictorial postage stamps and by advantages offered to mainland residents during the summer.

In 1885, some 300 acres in the vicinity of Russell Falls were proclaimed a reserve through the efforts of L. M. Shoobridge, and in 1893 the Tasmanian Tourist Association was formed. Members included J. W. Beattie and the government botanist L. Rodway, who was also in the Royal Society, the Field Naturalists' Club and a National Park Association. Beattie and Spurling of Launceston

Cadbury's chocolate factory at Claremont, 1921

began photographic work in the 1880s and promoted the scenic beauty of the colony by such means as lantern lectures.

The idea of national parks was forwarded as a result of publicity given the creation of the Yellowstone National Park in the United States, and in 1904, wilderness and the Tasmanian mind came together when the Tourist Association proposed that Crown land at Schouten Island and Freycinet Peninsula be reserved for native flora and fauna. There was a favourable response by the government and in addition a reserve was formed on part of Mt Wellington as well. Then W. E. Crooke took up the idea of creating a national park in the Russell Falls locality and at Mt Field. A National Parks Association came into existence under which 27 000 acres of reserve were set aside in the Cradle Mountain-Lake St Clair region at the beginning of the Great War. In 1915 also the National Parks Association succeeded in inducing the government to pass the Scenery Preservation Act. The park was officially opened in October 1917. In the meantime, the Tourist Association had got into financial difficulties and in 1914 a Government Tourist Bureau, under E. T. Emmett, was created.

In the north, Gustav Weindorfer, an Austrian, and his Australian wife, fell in love with the Cradle Mountain area and there constructed a chalet, opened in 1912. In the early 1920s the north-west coast newspaper the *Advocate* suggested the creation of a government reserve and when a northern branch of the Royal Society was established in 1921, it became active in supporting Weindorfer, but he became greatly discouraged and hurt by racist persecution during the Great War. In 1922 an area was proclaimed under the Scenery Preservation Act and a reserve of 158 000 acres gazetted. In 1925, 42 000 acres near the National Park were reserved as state forest, the largest area to that date.

Fauna had for long been under attack in the island though there was an Animal and Birds Protection Act passed in 1919; this was strengthened in 1928 after a number of hunting seasons dangerously reduced certain species. By 1930 there were two official bodies specifically orientated to conservationist or protectionist objects: the Fauna (Animals and Birds Protection) Board, and the Scenery Preservation Board. With the death of Weindorfer in 1932, a group of his friends bought his land and the Waldheim Chalet to forestall timber interests. By 1940 the Scenery Preservation Board had proclaimed about 470 000 acres of scenic reserve and the Fauna Board about 800 000 acres of fauna reserves, and the next year some 23 600 acres of Frenchman's Cap had also been proclaimed as a scenic reserve.

The administration of A. G. Ogilvie was marked by that premier's response to the Depression and to the necessity for Tasmania to be 'developed'—by which was meant the establishment of numerous labour-intensive secondary industries. It was this which led the government to advance the interests of the Hydro-Electric Commission more and more in the quest for industry. It appeared to Tasmanians of the time that, given their abundant supply of waterpower, there was no limit. Simplistic popular thinking perceived that the supply of rain and therefore water was endless and clean, compared with the smoke and grime associated with coal. Few if any considered that the spoliation of the countryside was other than minimal and a small price to pay for development and employment of the people. Could not Tasmania become a second Switzerland?

Behind this thinking lay a constant comparison—to Tasmania's disadvantage—with Victoria and New South Wales, whither so many young Tasmanians went. In the 1920s it was commonly thought that the state was victim of a brain drain. Certainly the population was increasing but slowly, from 191 000 (1911), 214 000 (1921), 223 000 (1931) to 242 000 (1941). The birth-rate was the highest in Australia but the state did not retain the Australia-wide proportion of the middle-years and younger age groups. Emigration still often exceeded immigration. This was so in census year 1911 by 4000 people and in 1941 by 6000, with a virtual balance between the two in 1921 and 1931.

Tasmania sought to share in S. M. Bruce's 'men, money and markets' slogan and in the island state immigration from Britain was handled as part of the Department of Agriculture in 1921 but in the first four years of the operation of the notorious Navigation Act there was an annual loss of 3500 people from the state and the natural increase of 1923–4 failed to overtake this deficit. The 1920s were bad years for Tasmania: the birth-rate in 1926 was the lowest since 1850 and the marriage-rate the lowest since 1918.

In the period between the wars Tasmanians maintained a great pride in their state but did not reap the benefits which they had been led to believe would flow from federation of the colonies. That federation was truly the creation of a free-trade zone and an island with Tasmania's disadvantages was bound to feel the draught. Not least were Tasmanians at once angered and proud by the constant passage of young sportsmen, and especially footballers, from their clubs to the top of the tree in the Victorian Football League. In the sporting world so important to so many Australians, Tasmania held its own perhaps only in the area of tree-felling and sports associated with the timber industry. The idea that the state was 'sleepy hollow' became something of a fixation and led Tasmanians probably to over-emphasize the attractions of Melbourne and Sydney and to over-value the importance of development and industrialization, although the work of the Hydro-Electric Commission in bringing the comforts of modernity to the ordinary Tasmanian could not be criticized by people who had known only wood-stoves and kerosene lamps.

As much as the Ogilvie administration accomplished in the Depression, it also shared in the difficulties of its predecessors at the hands of the Legislative Council. Many and varied were the things accomplished in the emergency years of the 1930s, but not among their number was checking the wide powers of the Council. In 1937, Ogilvie came into serious collision with that body when certain of its number objected to some of the premier's statements and rhetoric, jumping to the conclusion that Ogilvie was about to lay Tasmania in ruins—as if it were not in that state already—by his 'socialistic' measures. Thus the Council, convinced the state was in the grip of a madman, reduced an item in a Finance Bill involving an extension of 'socialism' in the mild form of government medical services being offered to the people in rural areas.

At this, Ogilvie promptly introduced a bill to settle the hash of the Council once and for all, the Council arguing that the matter in dispute formed no part of essential services to the people but was merely an extension of them. Ogilvie appeared determined to destroy the Council's power to frustrate the wishes of the people's house and observed that he would abolish the Council as soon as he could . . . but he did not.

Conferences commenced, Ogilvie assessed the feeling of the state and concluded it was conservative and, the question of the Finance Bill resolved, the matter was taken no further. Presently the death of Ogilvie and the outbreak of the war led to the whole matter being shelved.

7

Recognition

On the eve of the Second World War, Tasmania's population was approximately 244 000, of whom 123 000 were males and 121 000 females. They were distributed generally into the regions of the south (106 000), north (74 000), north-west (54 000) and west (10 000). The population of the City of Hobart stood at about 57 000 and that of the City of Launceston at 38 000, but between a quarter and a third of those numbers could be added to take account of surrounding local government areas which were integrated into the two principal and oldest settlements in the state.

By the late 1930s and early 1940s, the main regions were fairly clearly recognized by their industrial and rural economies, their centres of focus (Hobart, Launceston, Devonport and Burnie, and Queenstown), and their commercial radio stations and daily newspapers: the *Mercury* in the south, the *Examiner* in the north and the *Advocate* in the north-west, with the last devoting special space to the affairs of the mining-dominated west coast. These three main newspapers were principally owned by different interests (the Davies family, the Rolfe family and the Harris families respectively) which in turn also owned a number of radio stations. Other regional papers were published from time to time.

Such was the terrain of the rugged state and the limited strength of radio signals transmitted that people in the north and north-west could not readily hear southern radio stations, nor Hobart hear programmes emanating from outside its region. Radio station 7QT Queenstown catered for the west coast and 7DY Derby for the north-east. All commercial stations tended to broadcast similar material in terms of ubiquitous serials and radio plays and talent quests, and were linked to the local newspapers for news broadcasts. Brass-band music was popular.

In the north-west and to a lesser extent in the north, however,

Bass Strait was little impediment to clear reception from Melbourne. This orientated the areas more to the capital of Victoria than to the capital of Tasmania, reinforcing cultural and commercial links which had been present since the settlers of Van Diemen's Land began colonizing the Port Phillip District of New South Wales in the 1830s. Indeed, the Victorian Methodist circuit included Tasmania, and that religion was especially strong in the north generally. The Australian Broadcasting Commission catered for a minority audience from transmitters in Hobart and Launceston as well as directly from Melbourne. Its mass influence was slight though its cultural impact may have been substantial in some quarters, not least being the development of the children's Argonauts' Club in the early 1940s, and it influenced the outlook of some Tasmanian young people in a most important way by encouraging literary and artistic talent.

The newspapers and commercial radio stations, however, remained of great significance in regional terms. The price of apples (south) or potatoes and stock (north-west and north) could be principal headlines till the war came. The papers took themselves very seriously in editorial comment, continuing the nineteenth-century practice of the editor offering virtual sermons on the events of the day and their significance for the region. It may not have been a Tasmanian paper which began a leading article in late 1917 with 'As we have so frequently warned the Czar . . .' but it could well have been. Periodicals such as the *Weekly Times*, *New Idea* and *Women's Weekly* revealed to Tasmanians the wider world of interests relating to the man on the land and to women. Newspapers all had women's pages, offering the mixture of social gossip and sturdy common sense so characteristic of Australian women's journals. The *Listener In* from Melbourne was widely-read and filled its pages with Victorian wireless programmes, with comment on them and the radio stars of the day.

Display and classified newspaper advertisements reflected regional business and interests, offering the wares of local shops and stores, and answers to correspondents in rural areas were coloured more than a little by hints of local dramas and events, values and interests. A reader who sought to know whether old-age pensioners could legally back horses received the reply, 'Yes, and goats too'. Seasonal requests for fruit pickers or potato diggers reflected regional economies. Notices from time to time warned traders to be wary of accepting credit from certain people where marital relationships were evidently under strain, pleaded for the return of (winning) Tatts tickets unaccountably lost or allegedly purloined, and threatened or hinted at the administration of 'bootlace uppercuts' to enemies whose identity was gleefully recognized by readers in the know.

As elsewhere, numerous readers perused newspapers backwards, beginning with racing and football news and next moving on to items related to their districts. In country areas, newspapers

Tasmanian potatoes advertised by the Potato Marketing Board

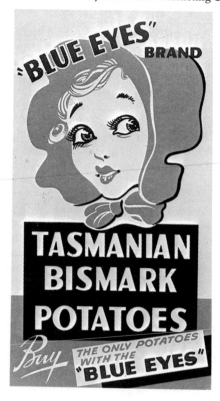

and mail were delivered late each day by mail cars or buses which threw out private mail bags as they went past.

The radio stations and newspapers in winter gave considerable space to football, the prospects for the season and predictions for the games, with eccentric experts such as 'Stab Kick' laying down the law. Regionalism was enormously strengthened by the presence of three main football organizations—the Tasmanian Football League (south), the Northern Tasmanian Football Association and the North-West Football Union, and there were smaller competitions elsewhere, such as on the west coast. In this region games were played on gravel surfaces because no suitable soil existed on the few naturally-flat areas. Local municipalities frequently had their own teams which were supported keenly, thus making it very difficult to alter the boundaries of local government areas.

Radio readers of teams were known to inject comments about players such as 'I hope he hasn't forgotten that load of wood he promised me for next week', a task made difficult in some areas when teams might consist of Smith (8), Brown (7), and a few players with other surnames. No public implications were drawn from such facts but in some areas the suggestion of inbreeding was clear, and certainly there was a common image on the mainland of Tasmanians having developed hillbilly proclivities. Some isolated parts of rural Tasmania were at once closeknit and deprived, and relationships close to incestuous were hinted at.

As elsewhere in Australia, religion was not seen as a powerful factor in everyday life. The pressures of colonial emergencies and hardship meant that the principal religions did not exert obvious power, although the Catholic church tended to retain its adherents more than most if church attendance is a criterion. Fringe religions such as the Christian Brethren and Gospel Hall flourished in the north-west, and Seventh Day Adventism attracted a few. This had unexpected results in some areas. There men accustomed to lend and pool farming machinery and labour found that their neighbours were unwilling to be available on Saturday but perfectly ready to lend a hand on Sunday, so that rural economies were threatened.

The antagonism and marked bigotry of some Protestants to Catholics strained social relationships, especially in places where clerics were sure and certain of their theological ground. The Irish origin of most Catholics had always led some Protestants to suspect them, and the views of Catholics on such matters as drinking and gambling were frowned upon by such as the Methodists, who held strong opinions on the sacred character of the Sabbath, the intrinsic sinfulness of drink and of what was said all too readily to flow from it.

Everywhere in the state, but especially in rural areas, the churches were of significance principally for marriages and deaths. About one-third of all marriages were conducted in the Church of England, another third in Catholic and Methodist churches (about the same number each) and 2–3 per cent in the Presbyterian church. Civil marriages were about 5 per cent. The clergy sighed when very nominal adherents sought a church wedding as a matter of right.

Weddings were occasions of great social importance, and the local significance (real or imagined) of the family and its outlook and income were revealed by the number of guests and the style of wedding breakfast. This could on occasion be taken to extremes and it was not unknown for rival in-laws to beggar themselves seeking to outdo the other in the variety and value of wedding presents.

Honeymoons inter-state, especially to Melbourne, could sometimes be afforded but more often the newlyweds travelled to Hobart or Launceston or toured the state by rail or motor coach. In the rural areas the return of the couple to their home—sometimes the parents' home—was frequently marked by an occasion known as a tin-kettling. Its origins in antiquity, this custom was very widespread in Tasmania and also practised on the Victorian goldfields in the 1850s. It tended to be predominantly male in its image and practice. A captain was appointed by general understanding and a date set for the occasion. Men and youths from all over the district gathered near the victims' house around nightfall and then proceeded to tin-kettle the couple out of their new domesticity by creating as much noise as possible. Men spent days beforehand loading shotgun cartridges which were to be fired off into the night sky, thereby risking and sometimes causing horses in stables to take fright and break out, to the fury of the owner and great delight of the tin-kettlers; men blacked their faces; it was known for old waggon wheels to have their hubs filled with gunpowder before being rolled down into the houses and detonated under verandahs with fearful results. When the man of the house emerged, it was the custom to invite his tormentors in.

The date of the tin-kettling was usually an open secret and the female friends and relatives of the bride provided food while the husband supplied liquor. Sometimes the tin-kettling festival was held out of doors in or near a barn and fires were lit for warmth and cheerfulness as the keg was broached, Cascade beer in the south, Boags in the north. One celebrator with a wooden leg got drunk, fell in a fire, set his leg alight and had to be put out by having buckets of water thrown over him. Sooner or later the groom attempted a short speech of welcome to his friends and the captain also spoke. Dancing and telling of stories marked the occasion, the music usually that of a piano, squeeze-box, violin or mouthorgan. In some cases the violin accompanied an exhibition of old jigs or 'steps'. Recitations were offered by those bold enough to think they could hold an audience. Not every newly-wed couple was offered a tin-kettling, but normally the occasion was an enjoyable one and basically marked the respect in which the host and his wife and their families were held.

By the late 1930s in Tasmania, few women had babies at home. The small size of the state and the social services work accomplished by the government ensured that maternity hospitals were readily available, though this did not preclude the mother-to-be undertaking arduous journeys by horse and cart to the nearest maternity hospital. Relatively affluent neighbours lent cars on occasion but more frequently mothers who lived in the country areas went to stay with relatives in a town when the birth of their baby was imminent.

Children in Tasmania were likely to be spoiled at home in their very early years but in the rural districts there still existed a good deal of exploitation of child labour during and after school days. The primary schools continued to be conducted in a very authoritarian manner and some young women still took up teaching through the 'monitor' system. Good teachers could always encourage promising children to go on to further education after they had turned fourteen, but many parents were indifferent or hostile to learning and sought to have their offspring enter the workforce as soon as possible; in some areas the local doctor was the only university-educated man who came into contact with the

Wrest Point Hotel, Hobart, 1945

people, and his encouragement of likely children was sometimes of crucial importance because he was listened to with respect, especially if he had successfully cured someone.

Entertainment was generally similar in Tasmania to that of other parts of Australia. Anzac Day was marked with great solemnity. Preceding this public holiday, schoolchildren were assembled to hear a returned man of the Great War spell out the values embodied in the word 'Anzac', and the names on the school honour roll might be read out, reminding children of the men who had fought. The Anzac Day services at local war memorials became sharpened in their significance as the war clouds gathered over Europe and a martial spirit was engendered.

Empire Day was also celebrated, though its solemn message of imperial unity was not so marked as that of Anzac Day, in part because in some areas it became associated with the presentation of apples and sweets to schoolchildren.

Sunday-school picnics and church anniversaries were also important occasions for many children. Forms of children's racing were mandatory at the picnics, frequently conducted at some picnic resort, and the award of book prizes at anniversaries enabled the transmission of the improving Christian message.

Tasmanians were as obsessed with films as anyone else. The term 'talkies' persisted in some areas well into the 1940s and the glamour of Hollywood lent colour to lives of picture-goers. The contrast between Hollywood's image of the world and the poor of the Derwent Valley was incredible, especially in the Depression, but all film-goers made a point of dressing well to go to the pictures. Everyone stood for the national anthem and films adjudged good were applauded as if the actors and actresses were on the live stage and could take a bow.

Among the popular sports, football, horse-racing and cricket stood pre-eminent, though many more attended football matches or watched contests on the turf than attended cricket fixtures. Cricket was very widely played and taken most seriously but was not a prominent spectator sport. Tasmania was not formally in inter-state cricket competition but its footballers were constantly sought by the big Victorian teams, who employed talent-spotters.

There were distinct regional variations in some other sporting occasions. In Hobart and the south, the Hobart regatta was marked out as it had been since the days of Governor Franklin. It was the occasion for picnics and relaxation and also a venue attracting the sideshows which travelled around Australia. The event was also customarily marked by the arrival in port of a warship; its ratings added the desired naval flavour to the entire occasion. The Hobart Agricultural Show was also a holiday, enabling farmers and graziers to offer their stock in competition, though the agriculturally richer north had the best exhibition of Tasmanian sheep and cattle at Launceston each spring. Newspapers pooled reporters and resources to offer readers an exhaustive list of winners and place-getters and details of exhibits. All Tasmanian centres of importance had such shows and stock sales which drew buyers from all over the continent from time to time, especially to purchase Midland sheep which continued to produce the best fine wool on the market.

Another form of entertainment was the Boxing Day and New Year carnivals which came to be associated especially with the north and north-west. Here was a series of occasions highlighted by bicycle races and pedestrian events. The Burnie Gift and Burnie Wheel Race enabled Tasmanian athletes to compete with Australia's best and, on occasion, visitors from abroad. Such holidays were a great day's outing in which thousands of people had picnics and gaped at or were induced to part with money to side-shows, ranging from throwing a penny on to a circle to boxing matches and freak shows. Harry Paulsen's troupe of pugilists and wrestlers dominated, and courageous, foolhardy or impecunious locals tried their skill, cunning and brute force against the visitors who sometimes included a faded star of the ring.

Tossing the sheaf was also popular at sports meetings, local men vying with each other to see who could toss a sheaf or a bag of hay the highest over a bar as it was pulled higher between two poles. Men also competed in 'stepping the chain' to see who most closely went an exact twenty-two yards as measured by the officials. Ploughing matches were also conducted, men using a favourite pair of horses to display their skills in ploughing straight and neatly.

Women's part in holidays tended to be confined to exhibitions of cakes and goods made at home, though some rode horses in show-jumping contests. Hunt clubs were confined largely to the Midlands, where the landscape permitted this recreation. Lesser mortals hunted rabbits with dogs and guns and possums with lights, and some kept ferrets which they released into rabbit burrows with nets set to catch the rabbits as they hurtled out to escape the ferrets. Capture of rabbits for their skins was a pastime and also a business for those who went into it in a big way. Rabbit skins were particularly sought in the winter, when the climate led to the production of thick pelts and high price, and traps might be set by the hundred. Poisoning was resorted to and the use of some, such as strychnine smeared on pieces of apple, led to the loss of animals other than rabbits.

Wood-chopping was the sport which reflected Tasmania more than anything else. From early in the century and before, areas in the forest country of the Huon district and the north were able to offer employment to men who became extremely skilful with the axe. Informal competition rapidly became formalized and champions emerged—Tasmanian axemen in the AIF competed in France and Belgium with lumber men from Canada, bushmen from New Zealand and their fellow Australian diggers who had worked in such timber areas as Gippsland.

In the Tasmanian form of competition, blocks of wood of particular measured thickness were nailed to permanent fixtures and there was intense competition as the contestants were counted

Tasmanian bushmen demonstrate their skills, 1927

down by voice to their handicap, the champions still standing nonchalantly by their blocks even as those first away were turning to begin the second side. Skill and timing as well as physical strength and fitness were all-important as the great chips flew and the crowd cheered on their favourite axemen.

As well there were tree-felling contests in which the axemen competed to mount trees by deftly inserting 'shoes', and when at the top, chop through the block there affixed. These contests were remarkable and dangerous exhibitions of a skill in which Tasmanians took great pride, where men literally put the final edge on their axe blades with razor strops, where a man would sometimes show off by raising his axe in one hand and, slowly bending his elbow, bringing it down to the tip of his nose, and where the axemen drew gasps from onlookers by descending from the 'trees' with incredible speed and ease. Local axemen's organizations publicized competitions in tiny centres as 'world championships' and indeed they possibly were, given the extent of the timber industry and the skill of Tasmania's axemen. Champion tree-fellers became folk heroes. Certain families were especially well-known, and their skills and iron nerve admired by all.

As elsewhere in Australia, death was the occasion for manifestation of local solidarity and solemnity. Irish-Tasmanians sometimes marked this by the conduct of wakes, where the body of the deceased was laid out in an open coffin and grieving relatives kept watch. Occasionally the mourning took on its ancient and traditional forms, with keening and outbursts of sorrow and the corpse addressed as if it still lived and could respond. There was no limit to the number who might attend a funeral, and hence respect for the deceased was measured by the number of people who came to the funeral if not the church service, itself normally a harrowing occasion. At the end of the 1930s, a funeral could bring an entire rural district of Tasmania to a halt. The carriers of the coffin were carefully chosen to represent family and friends and the chief mourners always specifically named in reports of the obsequies. Men uncovered their heads when the hearse made its solemn way to the graveyard. Relatives and acquaintances came from afar, not an easy thing when so many Tasmanians had connections on the mainland who were only enabled to attend a funeral at some considerable cost in time and money, for all were obliged to come by boat.

Those who attended such melancholy events were brought closer to their Tasmanian origins and their community by the sight of earlier gravestones and epitaphs, some of which most likely bore the same surname as the deceased. Epitaphs could be moving. At St Luke's, Richmond a man who died in 1838 had inscribed for him

> This world is a pleac full of crooked streets
> death is the market plaes weer all men meets
> if life was marchendyse as men could by
> he wuld live and soon must dey

Notices of deaths and funerals were commonly given in newspapers, and on local radio stations they were invariably preceded by the playing of solemn music which alerted the listener to bad news. Floral tributes were frequently the production of certain female members of families who perceived one of their most important roles in the making of wreaths. Usually constructed from the English flowers which flourished so well in Tasmanian gardens, these tributes were sometimes of quite exquisite design and pattern, a folk art. Trade unions and benevolent institutions such as the Oddfellows, Druids, Rechabites and church organizations went to great trouble to mark the death of a member by offering a wreath and making sure they had official representatives at the funeral, as an indication of respect for the departed.

As at weddings and funerals, the role of women in this society as a whole was fairly clearly demarcated, and though it was not unknown for women to work at harvest time alongside men, this was unusual because in rural areas work at most levels was still overwhelmingly based on the necessity of great physical strength. This factor, reinforced by social assumptions, meant that women were largely excluded. Girls were expected to become wives and mothers and housewives, or perhaps go into teaching or clerical work, or some of the new secondary industries which called for female labour in Hobart or Launceston. A certain number of girls always went nursing. The artistic learnt the piano or violin perhaps or were taught singing but the opportunities for advancement were extremely limited in such spheres. Commonly hobbies among girls were collecting and pressing flowers, sketching and painting, or crochet work and knitting which could lead to dressmaking, at least on a part-time basis. The gathering of clothes and objects for a glory box was taken for granted as something a young woman should do.

Most people still burnt wood in their domestic fires, despite the spread of electricity and use of gas in Hobart and Launceston, and the production of cooked food was regarded as a special female skill and indeed duty. A great deal of bread and jam was consumed by Tasmanians but basic diet was dominated by meat and cooked vegetables, followed by a pudding for the main meals. Dental health was bad and many people took it as a matter of course that they would wear false teeth. In urban areas where wood was purchased, theft of fuel sometimes occurred. One preventative was to let it be known that shotgun cartridges were carefully placed in auger holes in certain pieces of wood and concealed therein, so that the thief would experience unexpected action around the fire one night.

The principal and most valuable farm animal in Tasmania, at a time when tractors were still comparatively rare, was the Clydesdale draught horse. Stallions 'stood' at various places and their services were advertised; sometimes they were travelled to sire foals on good mares. The loss of a horse was catastrophic, and for men who depended so utterly on horsepower for their livelihood the decline of a favourite was a tragedy, such was the association between man and horse. There existed private and government veterinarians, but often farmers had inherited their own remedies and treatment, ranging from folk cures which had sometimes a basis in science, to deep common sense and empathy with their animals. Some men were renowned for their skill in treating certain animals as others were for repairing certain types of machinery such as the binder, and could be sent for from afar. To call in the vet, however, was to indicate that the animal was practically given up for dead or suffering from a condition which baffled the entire district.

The crucial importance of the horse led to the production of chaff and the giving over of areas of land to run horses and grow grass to feed them upon. Chaff was cut and grain threshed by itinerant chaff-cutters and threshing-machines or 'drums', in the 1930s brought to the site of the oaten hay stacks by traction engines, the route of which could be traced on the roads by the crushed blue metal which they created in their ponderous path.

Machine owners employed casual labour around a core gang, and the men camped near the machine, sleeping in the open or under whatever cover they could find. The work was hard, hot and dusty. Workers were supplied by the women of the property with breakfast, morning lunch, dinner, afternoon lunch and tea, all main meals centred upon large quantities of meat and tea, the men critically comparing the fare with that supplied by other owners locally or perhaps on the mainland where some men might have been shearing or droving or getting whatever employment they could. Tasmanian men who had travelled the mainland told tales of heat, distances and drought which were at once exotic and entrancing to the locals.

The supply of tea was kept up to the men in buckets all day long and careful tally was kept of the number of bags of chaff or grain produced. Payment was by cheque to the machine owner, though sometimes disagreements arose about whether the farmer should pay the feeder. This was the important individual who had the job of feeding sheaves into the machine at the proper rate so that it ran at maximum capacity and was not under-fed or so over-fed that a temporary jam could occur.

The growth of speedier transport was by 1939 beginning to break down the regional distinctions within the state, with their local cultures, but telephone books which listed subscribers under tiny districts reflected the fact that few people sought to communicate with those they did not know. Apart from those who emigrated to the mainland, people scarcely ventured out of their region, and a journey from the Huon to Hobart—perhaps a day trip by boat—or from Derby to Launceston could be a great event, long the subject of story. In many areas the only journey people made, except perhaps on the occasion of a death or some extraordinary reason, was to a weekly stock sale, though people might holiday with relatives in town or country.

In rural Tasmania, the other main impulse to move was probably to a clearing out sale, where a property was sold and the occupants decided to auction off unwanted equipment, furniture, goods and sundries. Here the auctioneer came into his own, a man equipped with knowledge of the area derived from long experience, a sharp sense of humour and the knack of shrewdly summing up what was worth pushing for sale, what was not. Like storekeepers, he knew who was worth money and who was not, and whom to trust. Settlement of accounts was normally on a seasonal basis.

The physical dangers which Tasmanians knew varied from region to region, and though the usual forms of infant and childhood diseases struck everywhere, they probably were more severe in crowded urban areas than in the country. Patent medicines continued to be widely taken, typically against forms of pulmonary diseases and 'female complaints'. There existed a stubborn belief in self-help, characteristic of colonials and people who still regarded admission to hospital as ominous in the extreme, even if they could afford it or were insured against illness. In city and country, old wives' tales and remedies abounded. People wore bags of camphor around their necks; scalding hot poultices were applied; copper bracelets were held to be effective against rheumatism; onions were rubbed on the soles of the feet against whooping cough; the water in which the brooklime was boiled was thought to be a general cure-all. Deaths and injuries caused by falling trees were not uncommon in some districts and of course could not be guarded against as disease, and, it appeared, neither could the affliction of infantile paralysis which struck Tasmania in 1937.

People everywhere had vegetable and flower gardens and fruit trees. Most fruit could be made into forms of wine, and vegetables were occasionally turned into alcoholic beverages by those who had inherited the recipes. Bees were kept in some regions and 'bee trees' sometimes yielded honey in the bush. Some Tasmanians manufactured a potent honey mead but little illegal moonshine was made. Some still manufactured their own candles, killed and scalded pigs and slaughtered sheep and cattle. Bread was made at home, and so commonly were boilings of jam, put into bottles with the tops cracked off neatly by application of a hot hoop of iron.

In the way of clothing, little was home-made in terms of the main over-garments, though a Tasmanian 'bluey'—a short thick overcoat—was favoured in some areas such as the west coast. Tasmanians except those of the more educated classes dressed in a way that could be described as old-fashioned. Women were not chic and smoked only if they did not care about being thought respectable, though it was smart in some circles. Mrs (later Dame) Enid Lyons recorded her Tasmanian astonishment and shock at seeing Mrs Ada Holman, wife of the NSW premier, smoking cigarettes, with Mrs Holman's initials on them.

Nearly all men wore a hat, especially for best. Tailor-made cigarettes were not yet in fashion generally. Men used cut-throat razors though some still wore beards. Boots, not shoes, were frequently worn, and kept in excellent order. Combination under-wear was common among men and youths, the flannel undershirt was usual and collar studs still in favour for attaching shirts when the owner got dressed up or sought to cut a figure.

Women's dress and advertisements reflected a conventional female role centred upon a 'smart' turn-out and beauty aids. Char-mosan Face Powder, for example, at 2s. 6d. for a big double box, was claimed to give instant youthful charm to the skin no matter how plain it might be, concealing and subduing faults and signs of age and staying on for hours. Subtle, chic and modern, it was said to take years from the looks of the beneficiary.

A svelte appearance was regarded as highly desirable, based on the ubiquitous corset, Berlei brand claiming to have achieved a major breakthrough in the 1920s by discovering that every woman belonged to one of five figure types. Corsets were offered for sale at 7s. 11d.. Floral frocks could be purchased for 55s. in the summer of 1939, and an OS navy floral frock with white lace front, collar and long sleeves for 35s. Ladies bloomers cost 1s. 6d. a pair, blouses 2s. 11d., tweed tops 1s. 3d., and princess slips, lace-trimmed with brassiere tops, were 2s. 11d.

Accessories such as hats, gloves and handbags were regarded as essential wear for most occasions and gloves could be bought for 11½d. a pair. Sewing machines were owned by most women and many advertisements suggested that a good deal of wearing apparel be made up at home, with rayon and cotton weave in vogue at 1s. 11d. a yard. One-piece bathing suits were the fashion and shorts had become popular, especially for beach wear.

On the whole, there were few serious signs of women's 'liber-ation' if the popular press is any indication, though it was thought quite proper to encourage girls and young women to ride bicy-cles, which could be bought for £1 down and 5s. a week. Birth-control devices had been generally available at least since the 1890s and on the eve of the war of 1939–45, advertisements on the women's page discreetly offered such items as Kareen, 'recommended by the medical profession', and 'medical goods'.

On the darker side of Tasmanian life in 1939, sinister murders were known to be committed, sometimes with entire districts closing ranks if it was thought necessary, so that even police might not pursue their enquiries very extensively. The people were generally suspicious of the police and a man on the run might receive much sympathy. Most families in the rural areas owned firearms and many districts knew which among their number was a crack shot and whether or not a man might use a rifle or shotgun seriously. Rape and murder were known, as was the destruction of the body by placing it in a stump or hollow tree and setting fire to it. Disputes might be held off or defused when it became known that certain families were quite capable of killing, so that interlopers removed themselves. Most quarrels, however, were settled privately, though animosities might smoulder for years in the form of feuds and pay-backs. Formal fights occurred. It would become known that a fight had been arranged, and friends of the opposed parties, together with curious onlookers who were careful not to take sides, would gather on a Sunday morning to see the two rivals square up and either fight to a finish or be persuaded after a few hits that honour was satisfied.

The isolation of Tasmania led in 1931 to a secessionist move in the south through the *Dominion* monthly magazine, but this got no further than other such impulses in states and areas of Australia which attributed their troubles to the federal government and its alleged disregard of local interests. Yet Tasmanians continued to feel different from other Australians and were certainly seen to be so, as are all islanders. A visit to Melbourne, and adventures there, would be the subject of anecdotes to impressed listeners for years. The constant emigration of local people and the insignificant immigration reinforced this sense of apartness and particular identity. A slightly defensive pride in coming from Tassie was emphasized.

There was an implicit continuity with the past which sometimes took explicit form. In 1951, 'A Call to the People', signed by high church dignitaries and the chief justices of the states, urged everyone to look to moral revival and to go forward together in the face of communist triumphs abroad and perceived unrest at

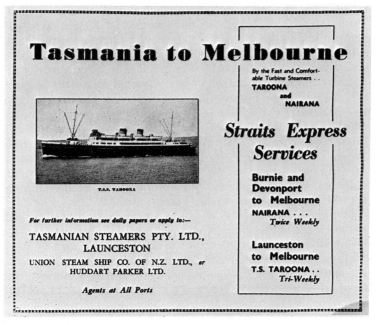

Tasmania to Melbourne

By the Fast and Comfort-
able Turbine Steamers . .
TAROONA
and
NAIRANA

Straits Express Services

Burnie and
Devonport
to Melbourne
NAIRANA . . .
Twice Weekly

T.S.S. TAROONA

For further information see daily papers or apply to:—

TASMANIAN STEAMERS PTY. LTD.,
LAUNCESTON
UNION STEAM SHIP CO. OF N.Z. LTD., *or*
HUDDART PARKER LTD.

Agents at All Ports

Launceston
to Melbourne
T.S. TAROONA . .
Tri-Weekly

Crucial links between Tasmania and the mainland, *c.* 1939

home. In the form of a leaflet, the Call was posted up on railway stations and the like. In Tasmania, across the uplifting passage which called 'on all our people to remember all whose labours opened this land to the uses of mankind . . .', and ending with 'Fear God, Honour the King', some wag wrote,

> They hitched us to their ploughs, my boys,
> To plough Van Diemen's Land.

This provocative quotation of part of a convict ballad recalling the violent origins of the state and society was unusual, however, although the countryside was thick with buildings which reminded people of their origins. Not least was the remains of the Port Arthur settlement, but its partial destruction in bushfires at the turn of the century was not greeted with sorrow. There were those who wished the place had been entirely consumed with flames, so that what was seen as a very recent and disreputable past might have its shame put out of sight as well as out of mind. Tasmanians did not wish to be reminded of their history and indeed took active steps in some cases to remove incriminating evidence from old documentary convict records. The rising generation was not encouraged in family history or genealogical research for fear of what might be discovered. A convict ancestor was nothing to be proud of or easily accepted. On the contrary, he or she was the subject of shame and a figure in a past over which it was desirable to draw a veil. Disinformation about family origins was common, but there was a great pride in respectable origins. The death in 1889 of one Robert Thorne was big news: he was born at Hobart Town in 1808 and was claimed to be the oldest native-born resident, with a brother who had been born at Port Phillip in 1803, his father a sergeant of Marines.

Five years later, in 1894, origins of a different kind were evoked: in the House of Assembly, George Crosby Gilmore, member for George Town and a lawyer, took it that he was accused by Allan McDonald, representative of North Launceston and an iron-monger, of being a transported convict and felt so incensed that he punched his accuser. This was said to be first fracas of the kind for twenty-five years.

Did this sort of thing confirm among Tasmanians the belief that they were indeed different from other Australians? Perhaps; it certainly helped. Those other Australians perceived Tasmanians sometimes with slight amusement as country cousins suspicious of the big city, people who took the precaution of sewing up their pockets or purchased money belts when venturing to Melbourne for fear of pickpockets, who were convinced that they would be taken down on the mainland, and who emerged from backblock areas where all kinds of curious customs prevailed.

But there was also conveyed, at the same time, an image of Tasmania as a little Merrie England, a picture cultivated and promoted by and for middle-class holiday-makers from the main-land, such as Martin Boyd. His was a picture of a more positive kind, one of fishing for blackback and of the 'apple isle', where there was a temperate climate and a relaxed life style. But Tasmania was not seen as the place where one sought employ-ment, except perhaps in certain specialized technical fields associ-ated with hydro-electric engineering or the mining industry.

On the eve of the war which began in 1939, then, Tasmanians

generally had developed a number of regional differences, economies and outlooks, highlighted by the spectacular difference between the life of a Queenstown miner and that of a grazier in the Midlands, close though they were as the crow flies. The big division was between town and country, but Tasmanians were rendered essentially one sub-group of Australians by the presence of Bass Strait. Some perceived that even a form of dialect or dialects had developed though this may be doubted if tested by any serious linguistic analysis. Yet there were odd expressions and words which identified people of Tasmanian origin.

The most common was the use of 'tissues' for cigarette papers and the form 'rum 'un' for a strange fellow. Other expressions are of obvious derivation, such as 'the other side' for the mainland of Australia and 'down on the front', an expression used by people in the hinterland for those dwelling on the sea coast. As well, various British dialect words were probably ossified in the island. Few folk tales from Home appear to have survived though some Irish-Tasmanians still told stories about 'the little people' and it is curious to note that in one area of the north-west, people on one side of a river performed dances with different steps to people on the other side, though the tunes were the same; and that in another area, the identical small bird was variously termed a chat, a nun, and a bullfinch by people from closely adjacent districts. Weeds and native grasses also had quite different names in different regions and districts, a fact which led to considerable confusion and misunderstanding.

Other expressions and terms included 'slewed' (become lost or confused); 'trinkling' (running water); 'setter' (a hard case); 'throw off' (to criticize); 'jag' (a small load drawn by horses); 'nointer', 'rooshun' (Russian?) or 'radical' (a mischievous child); 'shook' (stolen); 'planted' (hidden); 'cronk' (out of sorts or ill). 'Creek' was commonly pronounced 'crik', and 'sat' as 'sate' or 'sut'.

Some or indeed all of these may well have been common in other parts of Australia, as may have been the calls used to horses or bullocks in directing them, or numerous other calls used to attract animals. There were such exclamations of amazement as 'Hell and Tommy White', the common use of 'durst' for dare, a horse being so weak it 'couldn't pull the hat off your head', 'to run in the red steer' (to start a fire), 'to ride a razor bareback to London'; sayings such as 'go day come day, God send Sunday' and 'there's been many a good day's work wasted waiting for it to rain', and 'to rain pitchforks'. Other expressions are clearly based on songs, such as difficulties being referred to as 'a rocky road to Dublin'. Among children, counting chants and skipping songs existed in many variants and among adults there were numerous parlour games which appear, however, to be wholly inherited from Britain.

There was an extensive lore on snakes, of which Tasmania had in fact only three varieties, though they enjoyed numerous local names. Reptiles to be met with in Tasmania were all venomous, their bite ranging from venomous to extremely venomous indeed, depending on the type of snake, its size and the amount of poison it had the opportunity to inject into the victim. Some made odd sharp barking noises and could be extremely aggressive. The presence of a snake could be deduced from the strange piping notes of some birds, an unforgettable and hair-raising sound. Snake stories were of infinite variety and everyone could tell of numerous encounters and the strange conduct of the snake. Some held that the hoop snake definitely existed and had been witnessed bowling down hill with its head in its mouth upon unsuspecting travellers, people swore that they had seen snakes swallow their young, other tales recounted that a person once bitten would always be attacked again because the snake knew, that milk would entice a snake from beneath or in a house, that a snake could have its attention taken by a hat thrown down near it, that some snakes would attack a man on horseback, and that the bite of the 'goanna' (blue-tongue lizard) reappeared every twelve months in the form of sores.

Tasmanians were always perceived to be different, from the days when the Derwenter shearers were singled out by their style of clothing—tall hats and kangaroo knapsacks or 'Derwent drums'—when they went over the Strait during the period before the gold rushes. On the diggings, a few years later, inhabitants of Tasmania came to be distrusted and feared as the Vandiemonians, all labelled as convicts and ex-convicts, and up to all kinds of tricks and dishonesty, but showing particular satisfaction in contemplating their past and expressing loyalty to their island.

At a later period it was commonly stated, on the other hand, that Tasmanians were different because they were so friendly to visitors. This was probably true because the isolation and, when on their home ground, their apparently relaxed view of the world, gave them no reason to be antagonistic to other people who visited the state, providing those visitors did not criticize. It was based on a confidence which, however, was superficial. Edginess was another dimension always present. It was essentially based on Tasmania's history as it was commonly understood and the state's Cinderella relationship with the rest of Australia, but the Tasmanians did not take refuge in their past.

Hobart and Launceston and some of the older townships such as Ross, Campbell Town, Oatlands, Richmond and Sorell were obviously centred upon their historic buildings but the provincial settlements had never been much more than outposts, service centres for the surrounding pastoral areas and garrison towns when units of the British army occupied the colony. It was literally only a matter of minutes before one could be out of these centres and into the real Tasmania of mountains and hills, streams and rivers and extremely rugged country. If there was a bush or provincial image about the stereotype Tasmanian in 1939, it was partly because he or she reflected only too well the lack of urban modernity and the want of style, and the all-pervading bush.

Yet there also existed in the island state a very wealthy class which wielded power through the Legislative Council especially and which was far from being unsophisticated. These people were the gentry who had occupied some of the best pastoral land in the world from the very early nineteenth century and had been the confident masters and mistresses of a virtual slave labour force of convict workers. Educated, cosmopolitan and cultured in comparison with their fellow Tasmanians, they and their descendants enjoyed economic independence and a sense of security verging on arrogance which enabled them to travel widely, to educate their children among their social peers and to insist on forms of address, deference and conduct which were the striking opposite of the usual Tasmanian egalitarianism. Though their power declined as parliamentary democracy was ushered in, the experience and survivals from the past meant that still their interests were ensured representation and notice at all levels and substantial power through the institutions of the state, in the form of legislative and private organizations such as clubs and informal networks. But people of the wider world as they were, the gentry still stressed their loyalty to the island and remained first and

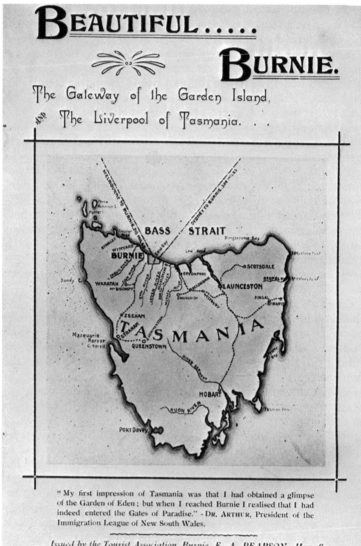

Burnie likened to Liverpool, *c.* 1907

foremost Tasmanians, which was only to be expected, considering how well they had done.

Federal members of parliament also stressed their common Tasmanianism over and above the interests of party from time to time. Differences on ideology could be submerged in order to promote Tasmania's interests. No mainland members of federal parliament took so much trouble to represent their state and make a point of being reported at home.

But over and above this sense of difference and attachment to the island state, the people continued as in the past to identify very strongly with the British Empire and the Old Country. In the last resort, and especially as Britain edged nearer to war, all the Australian states would depend they thought on Britain and its might, and the Royal Navy especially, for defence against the King's enemies. Had not Tasmanian schoolchildren for years gazed at maps of the world which had satisfyingly large areas coloured red?

But Tasmania was especially conscious of its vulnerability. It could always be cut off as no other state could be; the industrial upheavals and shipping strikes of the 1920s had forcibly brought this home. It reinforced its historic loyalty as nothing else could have, similarly to the case of New Zealand, where there prevailed a similar sense of Anglo-Saxon origin and isolation which fostered imperial feelings. There strongly persisted a sentimental and economic attachment to Home—not least strengthened by the apple market—which reached a point where Burnie could seriously be advertised as 'the Liverpool of Tasmania'. And above all perhaps this was immeasurably strengthened by the numerical dominance of the Church of England and the presence of English-born governors whose style was admired, and who offered a comforting link with safety and respectability. This was particularly important when it is realized that a youthful convict who arrived in 1853 was still alive in 1939. So close to its unrespectable origins was Tasmania on the eve of the Second World War.

8

Modernity

No more than any other Australians were Tasmanians surprised by the declaration of war against Germany in September 1939. Observers of the international scene shared the common gloom at the decline in collective security, the sinister pretensions and ambitions of Japan as they perceived how that nation thrust its way into the areas of European and American interests in China, the belligerence of Italy and the determination of Herr Hitler to create the Third Reich.

Tasmanians sought to enter the Empire Air Training Scheme, the navy and the AIF, and by 1940 the sons and relatives of the men who had gone to the Great War were again on their way to the Middle East. There they observed the same sights as had their predecessors, though possibly the superior quality of officers and the experience gained from the events of 1915 in Egypt led to more sensible recreation for the men than had been the case twenty-five years earlier.

At home the interim government of Edmund Dwyer-Gray was replaced by that of Robert Cosgrove, and he was to continue as premier of the state for the duration of the war and beyond it. Labor's hegemony showed no sign of being threatened in the late 1930s and still less once the war had begun.

As elsewhere in Australia, the war created great demand for labour, and unemployment was reduced at the same time as the government in Canberra took steps to impose controls on prices. When Joseph Lyons died in office in 1939, he was succeeded as Prime Minister by Arthur Fadden who then quickly made way for Robert Menzies. The new leader of Australia, however, did not exemplify the leadership thought appropriate in the crisis of war. Especially in Tasmania were there those who concluded that the conduct of Menzies had been less than that of a loyal lieutenant to the ailing Lyons. Upon the late Prime Minister's death, his body was returned to the island which he frequently said he should never have left in the first place. Greatly-loved, he was buried at Devonport in a grand ceremony when his body was conveyed thither in a warship.

In 1940–1, all eyes were fixed on Europe and the war there as newsreels especially came to reveal the nature of modern war and the German methods of blitzkrieg. One evening children listening to the wireless programme for youngsters heard it interrupted with the grave announcement that German troops were now at the gates of Paris, and soon film news revealed the air onslaught on the Old Country. In 1941 as Britain was revealed to be standing alone against the enemy, Tasmanians were among those members of the second AIF sent to Malaya and the East Indies, to strengthen the Empire's defences in that quarter. The Tasmanians of the 2/40th Battalion were destined to be captured and were imprisoned for the duration of the war by the Japanese.

Tasmanians gaped at visiting American ships and service personnel in 1942, the strangeness and romance of the new allies rendered greater by their rare appearance compared with the troops on the mainland; they farewelled local soldiers and heard their conduct measured against that of the imperishable Anzacs, and became accustomed to shortages and rationing in the course of time. Slit trenches were dug, gas-producers were employed on vehicles, ration books issued and car headlights dimmed by application of cardboard shades. A brown-out came into existence. Schoolchildren were made aware of war through movie films, the emotion of teachers when a son was killed or captured or posted missing, and above all by the obvious feelings with which Anzac Day was marked by adults. The one day of the year conveyed a mixture of urgency, tears, fear and the will to win the war which it was never to transmit again.

For the next of kin of Tasmanians taken prisoner of the Japanese there was to be little heard, though many rumours circulated of radio messages sent out by the Japanese authorities or cards said to be have been received. An ominous one stated, it was claimed, that the soldier was well but wished he were with his father in Carr Villa—but Carr Villa was the Launceston cemetery site.

Price and production controls enabled some people to do well from the war. Economically, the conflict was not generally a disaster for Tasmanians and goods in short supply were usually available on the black market or by devious means. Thanks to the presence of tens of thousands of American servicemen—all conscripts—and possibly the influence of General Douglas MacArthur on the new Labor Prime Minister, John Curtin, there was no bitter upheaval over the question of compulsory military service as there had been in 1916 and 1917. The further the war went, the more powerful did Labor become and it had a great electoral triumph in 1943 when Curtin and the party associated themselves with rolling on to victory after the tide had turned in New Guinea by the end of 1942.

In Tasmania, Labor won three of the five seats and all three senate positions but there was considerable controversy on the question of whether the war should be financed by uniform taxation or by national credit. The Labor *Voice*, conducted by Dwyer-Gray, feared that a system of uniform taxation would ruin a disadvantaged state such as Tasmania, and R. G. Menzies sought to fan the flames of dissent by congratulating the editor on his stand, and the *Voice* quietened down somewhat.

Tasmania was a very tiny cog indeed in the war machine, but in 1942 it had become notorious or famous, depending on whether one applauded the legislative Council: in that year it alone among all the Australian legislative councils rejected a plan formulated by Robert Cosgrove whereby a referendum on state powers would be avoided by the states agreeing to hand over certain temporary authority to the federal government. This action precipitated the 1944 referendum which was rejected, thus confirming (if that were required) the Legislative Council in a sense of its superior wisdom.

The population of Tasmania in 1933 was 227 599. When the next census was taken after the war in 1947, it had risen to 257 078, to 308 752 in 1954, and 350 340 in 1961, figures below the national average yearly increase. In 1971 there were 390 413 people in the state and in 1981 this had increased to 418 957. Only in the period 1947–54 was the rate of population increase in the island above the national average, when there was substantial immigration from the Netherlands and the Baltic states. Tasmania however retained the highest proportion of Australian-born (90 per cent) of any state. In 1966, for instance, non-British European population was only about 3.5 per cent, compared with Victoria's 12 per cent. Of the overseas foreign-born, nearly half were

German or Dutch and more than half of the immigrants continued to arrive from the United Kingdom.

In short, even the huge intake of immigrants into Australia in the period immediately after the war had a limited social impact on Tasmania. The population of the Hobart area increased considerably faster than that of the north or north-west in the 1960s but the four main regions of the state remained distinct, though the west was in population decline.

Also in decline was the number of Tasmanians occupied in primary production. In 1933, primary producers were 33 per cent of the population but in 1961 this figure had declined to 11 per cent only. In the 1960s, secondary industry came to account for no less than 60 per cent of the total value of production. Farming became more efficient in the post-war boom years, following indications of this trend during the war when in order to victual troops, vegetable canning began and fruit processing was encouraged. Furthermore, the war in Korea and the leap in wool prices in 1951 provided capital for farm investment, and great expansion and increased efficiency occurred in the mid-1950s to the mid-1960s. In general, farming output doubled after the war at the same time as the labour force employed contracted by more than one-third.

Patons & Baldwins knitting factory, 1945

In the early 1950s, the value of Tasmanian factory production first exceeded the production value of its primary resources: by 1961 about 23 per cent of the Tasmanian workforce was engaged in manufacturing, less than in Victoria (31 per cent) but more than in Western Australia (18 per cent).

It is interesting to note that whereas in Victoria Melbourne accounts for about 80 per cent of that state's secondary industry, in Tasmania the figures for 1961 were 37 per cent for Hobart and 22 per cent for Launceston. These figures reveal the continued high profile of non-capital cities in Tasmania and hence the persistence of the strong regionalism for so long a characteristic of the state and colony. Only Queensland among the other states had a similar regional pattern.

Transport and communications also changed radically in the post-war period, especially with the new era of drive-on and other specialized ships which began with the *Princess of Tasmania* in late 1959. During the period 1954–64, the quantity of cargo handled in the state nearly doubled and enormous improvements were made in sealing roads all over the state and adapting them to modern transport. Roads partly based on ancient Aboriginal tracks and the easiest path for horse or bullock teams, were straightened, old settlements bypassed and modern highways pushed through to facilitate the speed and easy travel of cars and semi-trailers. In the bush, chain-saws and caterpillar-track vehicles took over from axes, horses and sheer manpower.

Side by side with the changes involved in the economy went advances in the field of health. A division of government devoted to the study and eradication of tuberculosis was established in 1944 and earlier arrangements for treatment consolidated in the Tasmanian Chest Hospital, enlarged in 1945, the same year as voluntary X-rays were introduced, to be followed by compulsory X-rays in 1950. The mentally ill were also much better treated than hitherto with the passage of the Mental Health Act in 1963, based on the findings of a British Royal Commission.

In the field of education too changes occurred. The state system continued to attract the great majority of pupils, but whereas in New South Wales, some 26 per cent of children attended private schools, in the island state it remained at only about 17 per cent. In 1944 the school-leaving age was raised to fifteen (subsequently to sixteen), and in the late 1950s sweeping changes occurred when academic high schools were modified and a new system of comprehensive schools instituted, with matriculation colleges for those wishing to go on to higher education. This was another example of a former trend in a state where distances were not great and the advantages of centralized education more apparent than elsewhere.

Throughout this period of post-war economic boom, however, Tasmanians continued to leave their island in large numbers: in 1954 for example, 20 per cent of the Tasmanian-born lived on the mainland, of whom two out of three were in Victoria. Tasmania's proportion of the total population of the nation continued to go down and by 1982 was at only 2.8 per cent of the total. In 1981–2, Australia as a whole grew at the rate of 1.66 per cent of population whereas the figure for Tasmania was 0.67 per cent, the lowest of all the states and territories.

On the other hand, the birth-rate in Tasmania continued to be the highest in Australia except for the Northern Territory. The net reproduction rate for 1981 in Tasmania was 0.99, the lowest 0.85 for South Australia. Fertility rate appears to be associated with lack of urbanisation as well as a population which includes an adequate number of women in the child-bearing years. In 1981, Tasmania recorded the lowest urban population in Australia (except for the Northern Territory) at 75 per cent compared with the Australian average of 86 per cent. Population enumerated by the census as dwelling in rural areas was 25 per cent (only the Northern Territory was higher) compared with the Australian figure of 14 per cent overall.

In religious terms, the state remained a bastion of Anglo-Saxon protestantism, the large number of Dutch immigrants re-establishing an old pattern of religion by settling in large numbers on the Methodist north-west coast, and south of Hobart. In the 1960s, about 44 per cent of the people numbered themselves as Church of England, about 20 per cent put down 'Catholic' or 'Roman Catholic' in the census, 14 per cent being Methodists and 6 per cent Presbyterians.

Following the establishment of the Commonwealth Grants Commission before the war of 1939–45 and the creation of a class of claimant states within the federation, Tasmania gained from the granting of federal money on the whole. The successful imposition of direct tax by the federal authority in 1942 was to

Map of Tasmania *c.* 1980, showing local government areas

prove particularly important for Tasmania because it took the state government off the taxation hook to a large extent. More and more the effective power of the purse strings was removed from the local parliament and taken by Canberra, so that by the 1960s, some 80 per cent of Tasmania's revenue was derived from federal grants, and only 20 per cent from state taxes and imposts.

Despite this or because of it perhaps, Tasmania retained a distinct and jealous sense of individuality which was associated with the conviction that industrially it lagged always that little bit behind the rest of Australia, even with the new developments and impressive modernization which occurred typically in the 1960s. How was Tasmania to catch up? Through the workings of the Hydro-Electric Commission, the miracle to be wrought by pouring money and expertise into it and promoting hydro power as a harbinger of development and a type of cargo cult.

Certainly secondary industry there was, and with it further trade and the concomitants of commerce. Earlier in the century there was discerned the eagerly sought benefits of industrialization in the form of power for carbide works as well as the Electrolytic Zinc Company, woollen mills and the impressive works of Cadbury-Fry-Pascall at Claremont. In 1941 newsprint was first produced at Boyer, in 1955 the Bell Bay aluminium plant was opened in the north, in the early 1960s uneconomic west coast railways were closed at about the same time as the long-planned Tasman bridge was opened over the Derwent at Hobart to replace the 'temporary' floating bridge hastily put in place during the war, and more firmly linked the eastern shore with the central business district. In 1968 the Batman bridge across the lower Tamar was opened, in 1971 Associated Pulp and Paper Mills began using a very extensive plant at Wesley Vale near Devonport, and a $9 million expansion programme at Bell Bay, by Comalco, was completed. In 1973 Australia's first legal casino at Wrest Point in Hobart sought to attract the tourist dollar and in 1975 the federal government took over the railways of the state.

Tourism became more and more a big business, with the establishment of extensive new offices in Hobart and elsewhere in Australia, and in 1980 a seven-year plan to develop the convict ruins at Port Arthur, physically by far Australia's largest reminder of its origins. Perhaps of equal or even of greater ultimate importance for the state's economy and identity came to be the work of the National Trust in seeking to retain historic buildings for posterity, and the passage of legislation in the early 1950s designed to safeguard the superb documentary records of the colony and state.

But some factors continued historic impulses. For instance, in

LAKE PEDDER
CAN NOW
BE SAVED
UTG

Authorised by C. Harwood 70 Queen St. Sandy Bay Tas
Printed by Swiftprint 30 Queens Rd Melbourne

The attempt to save Lake Pedder, *c.* 1972

1948 the Legislative Council decided to deny Supply to the government because the premier, Robert Cosgrove, was said to have been involved in a scandal, though found innocent. The subsequent election for the House of Assembly was fought on the issue of 'the Council or the People'. The government lost one seat but very little in the way of overall support and was enabled to continue in office with the assistance of an Independent.

The Council, however, continued to hold a gun to the head of the Assembly; because its powers were never made crystal clear, the Council was not obliged to go to the country though the House might be, and the boundaries of its nineteen single-member electorates were such that their size varied considerably.

From time to time there arose murmurs that the Hydro-Electric Commission had become a vested interest and a state within a state, and evidence emerged that its recommendations were not always fully explored with serious purpose on the floor of parliament. As the conservation movement gathered strength, despite the failure to prevent the flooding of Lake Pedder, it appeared that the Commission tended to over-state its case, and give an impression of arrogance and being above and beyond serious criticism when people sought to question it.

In 1969, Labor lost office when Kevin Lyons, an Independent and son of the late Prime Minister, supported the Liberals. It was later returned under the leadership of William Neilson. Then in 1977, Douglas Lowe became premier, to be succeeded by Harry Holgate in 1981. Then Labor lost favour with the people again and the Liberals under Robin Gray took office.

A good deal of this was the result of conflict concerning the Hydro-Electric Commission; its plans for further expansion began to run into opposition. Critics stressed that more secondary industry did not automatically imply more employment and income because computerization and automation were becoming common. It was pointed out that the Hydro-Electric Commission could not go on expanding for ever because the supply of rivers must run out—and what would happen then? There were those who, appreciative of the efforts of the Commission, yet felt that it had done its main work. Of some further weight was the claim that tourism, for many years a most important money-spinner for Tasmania, would not be encouraged by production of more dams and powerlines and canals, and that wilderness areas should be safeguarded for future generations on grounds both economic and aesthetic.

With conflict about a new dam above or below the Olga River in the west of the state, a plebiscite was held which included many apparently deliberately spoilt ballot papers and write-in remarks favouring no more dams. The Legislative Council rejected the government's proposal for a Gordon-above-the-Olga scheme, Dr Bob Brown emerged as champion of the 'greenies', and the inflammatory suggestion was made that many conservationists led idle and useless lives. The battle became Australia-wide and drew a good deal of attention overseas. The south-west was placed on the World Heritage list, to be safeguarded at all costs, the new state Liberal government threw in its lot with the Commission, internationally-known and nationally-respected figures opposed the spoliation of the area and in 1981 a major archeological discovery of Aboriginal stone tools and animal bones was reported located in a cave site on the banks of the Franklin River in the threatened area. The Labor party at the federal level fell out with the state party, members of which included people who considered that the future of the Commission was closely tied to their future too. The new federal Labor leader, Bob Hawke, pledged that a win for his party would mean the end of the damming of the Gordon. Hawke won the federal election convincingly, the High Court found for the federal authority and Tasmania was promised compensation by the incoming Labor government in Canberra.

Tasmanians gave vent to their feelings about the whole matter by voting in Liberals in all federal seats as they had in 1975, though many groups, including the state's own National Parks and Wild Life Service, had queried the political motives and competence of the Commission. The conservation interest received enormous assistance and publicity from all over the world. The arrest of many people, including very prominent Tasmanian citizens, for alleged trespassing only served to bring the Commission and its statistics, rationale and conduct under ever-closer examination.

The entire transaction was one of the few, and possibly most important, cases where 'development' received a salutary check and states' rights were defeated. The hydro-electric 'white gold' of which so much had been made by Robert Cosgrove and then Eric Reece, as Labor premiers, accomplished wonders when

Conflict with the Hydro-Electric Commission, 1981

comparison is made with the life of the ordinary Tasmanian in the days before the Commission brought electricity to virtually every home in the state. The need to question it was, however, probably as much the fault of various governments' enthusiastic but simplistic attitudes as of the Commission's management and conduct.

For many years the various census return in Tasmania listed no Aborigines, but it became a sign of new times and problems when Tasmanians who so identified themselves appeared in the 1970s. Partly due to the guilt of European Tasmanians about what their ancestors had done to the Aboriginal people, the struggle of Tasmanian Aborigines for recognition was not strongly resisted when it came to the disposal of skeletal remains. Some people, however, objected to the ritual cremation of the unique remains of Trugannini on the grounds that the Aboriginal people had responsibilities to people on earth other than themselves, and that in the future the welfare of humanity might be improved by scientific discoveries related to Aboriginal remains.

By 1984, Tasmanians' interest in their past and how they came to be what they were was greater to a degree than it had ever been. Unresolved problems of the past opened fissures in the grounds of the present. The environmental movement, interest in Aboriginal culture and a preoccupation with genealogy all found very rich areas in which to flourish.

The people of the island had always been obliged, whether they liked it or not, to develop a sense of place and a perception of the many landscapes to be found in the island. The past dictates the present and false perceptions of history distort the lens through which the present is refracted. Painters had always found in Van Diemen's Land/Tasmania a landscape which was irresistible, though it first came to be shaped in the painter's eye with English assumptions and techniques. Similarly, early writers of prose and poetry wrote essentially as immigrants and celebrated the Empire and the land they had left behind.

During the 1950s things began to change. The work of the National Trust together with increasing numbers of young men and women enabled to attend university and be stimulated by the serious study of history and literature, assisted the development of new writers who put down in prose and verse what they felt were fitting subjects for scrutiny and reflection. They willy-nilly distilled a perception of their island, so that such as Vivian Smith and Christopher Koch were observed by Douglas Stewart on the *Bulletin* and Kenneth Slessor to be reflecting a vision of the island and its people. Gwen Harwood and James McAuley also have written verse which owes something to the Tasmanian scene, and there are currently other poets and prose writers who may be undertaking journeys of personal exploration and identity in their writing as well as offering perceptions of a wider significance.

Side by side with such serious writing has emerged more popular work, now casting a much wider net in terms of interest than the old preoccupation with shadows over Tasmania cast by the convict system and the hangman's noose. Local histories and memoirs appear to be published by the hundreds at first sight when the observer is confronted by them and their fellow slim volumes, pamphlets and historical guides in Tasmanian book-shops. There appears a virtually unslakeable thirst for knowledge of the past, no doubt impelled in part at least by the increasing anonymity of Tasmanians as individuals as they are caught up like everyone else in the computer age, automation and high technology which mark a new industrial revolution.

But the varied landscapes of the island remain. James McAuley in recent years was able to describe a Tasmanian scene which, unknown to him apparently, had been the precise one described 125 years earlier by Louisa Anne Meredith. Depictions in prose and poetry of Tasmania cannot truly be said to represent a sense of gusto or mastery in relation to the landforms and history, though enthusiasts have sought to present it so, whether from horseback, bicycle, car or aeroplane. The climate of much of Tasmania may, can and does kill the unwary; in its violent and mindless moods the observer is swiftly cut down to size. It is this perhaps which Professor Leonie Kramer has described as the 'pervasive melancholy' of the island's atmosphere. This strikes the returning exile—a common Tasmanian figure—very forcibly, and doubtless is caused by a combination of muted colour and light and the forms of the landscape, reinforced by an insight into the impact made by the European invader-colonist. The traveller in many parts of Tasmania can still only too readily conclude that he is standing alone on an empty stage.

The political ideology which came to dominate the Australian colonies also had an impact in Tasmania. This was a form of liberalism, brought particularly by the urban English immigrant and characterized by the optimisitic conviction that the government must step in from time to time to ensure that all should have an opportunity to prosper, and that none save the quite undeserving should suffer as the result of chance misfortune or aggressive and calculated exploitation.

Great attention was always paid to developments in Britain, and Tasmanians were particularly apt to be influenced by progressive British patterns in legislation and outlook, especially in health, working conditions and education. The notice taken of the 1944 British Education Act was typical. When the first parliament asembled in 1856, for instance, the conventions and customs and rules of procedure of the House of Commons were slavishly adhered to, with local members very familiar with the standard British works on the conduct of parliamentary debates.

With hindsight it may be possible to argue that self-government was introduced too early in the tiny colony of Tasmania, and that it could not and would not work effectively unless the wealth of the island and its population increased substantially. The charge was later frequently to be made that Tasmania was over-governed, and supported too many public servants. There was and is, however, a minimum number required to discharge the obligations of modern government as it has developed and been accepted. Clearly the extent of this minimum number is the subject of argument and disagreement, and may embody vested interests which can endanger the people's respect for local and state administrations, but a minimum number there certainly has to be. This was bound to be a higher proportion of the number of people as whole than in other more populous colonies and states, but this fact does not of itself destroy the necessity to staff the departments of state.

As in the other colonies and states, substantial power was wielded by the Legislative Council, and it could be held that such was this power that the basically democratically-elected people's House or House of Assembly grew inured to and came to accept as universal wisdom the idea that there should be a body charged with putting the brakes on the wishes of the voters as they emerged in the decisions of the representatives of the sovereign people.

It has been a theme of Tasmania's history that the Council

actively thwarted the wishes of the House, savaging its legislative proposals more than a little. The problem of agreeing with the necessity or desirability of such a class of guardians is first, that they by their existence insult every member of the House by implying that it, and the people who elect it, cannot be trusted; and second, that there is no logical reason why a further check on guarding the guardians should not be necessary.

The history of Tasmania's occupation by Europeans is one of transplanted Britons clinging to and emulating the institutions of the colonizing authority, modifying them only insofar as allowed by forces of the market place and those who exercise hegemony. The discontent with federation and its result reinforced Tasmania's reluctance to accept direction from Canberra and from the mainland generally. The state was not affected by immigration of non-British peoples to anywhere near the same extent as other states and hence its vision of the world and of itself continued relatively unaffected by the new metropolitan image formed elsewhere in Australia.

References

This *Short History of Tasmania* is based on despatches transmitted between the governors of Van Diemen's Land/Tasmania and the Colonial Office, *Journals and Printed Papers* of the Parliament of Tasmania, newspapers, periodicals and theses held in the Morris Miller Library of the University of Tasmania. Also used were:

Australian Dictionary of Biography, Melbourne, 1966 to date

Bennett, S. C., *Federation*, Melbourne, 1975

Davies, J. E. (ed.), *Atlas of Tasmania*, Hobart, 1965

Davis, Richard, *Eighty Years' Labor: the ALP in Tasmania, 1903–83*, Hobart, 1983

Green, F. C. (ed.), *A Century of Responsible Government 1856–1956*, Hobart, n.d. [1956]

Lake, Marilyn, *A Divided Society: Tasmania during World War I*, Melbourne, 1975

Murphy, D. P. (ed.), *Labor in Politics: the State Labor Parties in Australia 1880–1920*, St Lucia, Qld, 1975

Robson, L. L., *A History of Tasmania*, volume I: *From the earliest times to 1856*, Melbourne, 1983

Smith, Vivian, *Tasmania and Australian Poetry*, Hobart, 1984

Tasmanian Historical Research Association, *Papers and Proceedings*, 1951 to date

Tasmanian Year Book, 1966 to date

Townsley, W. A., *The Government of Tasmania*, St Lucia, Qld, 1976

Index